CW00358067

The
Great Western Railway
in
WEST CORNWALL

Alan Bennett

© Alan Bennett
Runpast Publishing
ISBN 1 870754 12 3
March 1988, Reprinted 1990, 1995

Typeset by
Alphaset
65A The Avenue,
Southampton
SO1 2TA

Printed by
The Amadeus Press Ltd,
Huddersfield
West Yorkshire

Published by
Runpast Publishing
10 Kingscote Grove, Cheltenham, Glos. GL51 6JX

Introduction

Until the early 1960s West Cornwall was host to three railway termini, at Helston, Penzance and St Ives. Together they served the entire western peninsula from the Lizard in the extreme south, westward around Mounts Bay to Lands End and thence to the north coast and St Ives. The Helston branch, the last to open, (1887) closed to passengers in 1962 and to goods not long after. Penzance and St Ives still retain their rail services, the latter however, holding on to a precarious existence linked mainly to summer tourist traffic.

Fish, tin and copper may have been Cornwall's traditional toast to the sources of work and welfare but by the time that the railway had established itself locally the emphasis had moved to fishing, agriculture and, significantly, tourism. The story here is with the history and development of the railway in West Cornwall and specifically with its impact on these three industries so closely involved with its progress. Hopefully the links between railway and community will emerge in such a way as to make clear the nature of their interdependence.

West Cornwall's story shares a certain amount of common ground with many other communities in Britain influenced by the growth of the railway system, but, there is much that is definitive of the area itself, not least its geographical position. Interplay within the three principal but contrasting aspects of the local economy contributed much to overall identity of the district in cultural as well as social and economic terms. Railway initiatives in response to local conditions also made for character and diversity in operational matters. The relationship between the different forms of transport, in particular rail and sea, again adds to the story. Penzance, of course, has never lost its identity as a busy trading port and this has had a certain degree of influence over the character of the town and district as a resort.

Finally, West Cornwall can make a good claim to its part in the creation of the 'legend' of the Great Western Railway, especially in its close associations with tourism and the image of the 'Holiday Line'. The area was always considered special, unique even, by GWR publicity and, perhaps, if for no other reason than it being the very end of the line, West Cornwall has a special identity well known to people throughout Britain. Having once visited the area few people could easily forget their journey and its impact. Not many parts of Britain can offer the scenic attractions of the railway ride into the far West. Gliding along the shores of Mounts Bay into Penzance with St Michaels Mount standing sentinel nearby, or hovering, it seems, on the very cliff edge on the branch to St Ives, it soon becomes apparent that the railway has become a familiar and well loved feature of the landscape itself.

'Bulldog' class No. 3418 *Paddington* entering Penzance on what is believed to be the inaugural working of the *Cornish Riviera Express* on 1st July 1904.
Courtesy of Cornwall County Museum, Truro

Contents

Chapter One
The Early Years

By the mid nineteenth century Cornwall's growing trade needed a faster and more reliable means of transport than that traditionally provided by sea. Shipping was too often subject to long and costly delays, as *The West Briton* reported in April 1852:

'The want of a railway between this county and London has seldom been more severely felt than during the last two months. A continued prevalence of easterly winds during that period has almost completely obstructed the passage of vessels up Channel, and innumerable cargoes have been detained off the coast without the possibility of being discharged. We believe that no fewer than a hundred vessels are at present lying to the west of the Lizard being unable to weather the point; and Falmouth harbour and the other ports on the south coast are all crowded with shipping, waiting for a favourable wind to proceed on their voyage to the east.'

The railway was the key to progress within the county, and by mid century definite steps had been taken to ensure its presence.

The Hayle Railway was the first to serve West Cornwall. This company was incorporated in June 1834 and opened to traffic in stages from December 1837 to June 1838. It was built to serve the mining industry; to link the mining district inland around Camborne and Redruth with the north coast ports of Hayle and Portreath. From Hayle the line extended to Redruth over a distance of 9 miles 44 chains, providing a valuable link between these two important centres of trade. With its various lines to Tresavean Mine, Portreath harbour, Roskear and North Crofty the company worked a system amounting to 17 miles 15 chains overall.

In building its line, the Hayle Railway made particular use of inclined planes. Two of these were in use between Hayle and Redruth whilst two others were features of the lines to Tresavean and Portreath. The first on the Hayle-Redruth route was to the east of Hayle itself near the village of Angarrack. The Angarrack Incline climbed eastward to high ground on a gradient of 1 in 10 for 30 chains. Locomotives worked on all other parts of the line east of Angarrack, with the exception of the Portreath Incline, but they only worked westward to Hayle on the Angarrack Incline from 1843 onwards. The stationary engines operating on the inclines worked in conjunction with the locomotives. Further east, between Gwinear Road and Camborne, Penponds Incline involved yet more negotiation, this time on a gradient of 1 in 22 for half a mile.

Freight traffic worked in connection with the mining industry was of greatest importance to the Company but passenger services also became a feature of the line. From May 1843 a regularised passenger service between Hayle and Redruth was introduced. Intermediate stations were provided at Copperhouse (Hayle) Angarrack, Gwinear, Penponds, Camborne and Pool. With both its freight and passenger interests bringing valuable return, the Hayle Railway showed the potential for much more ambitious projects to follow.

A vital first stage in the development of railway activity locally was completed on 3rd August 1846, when the West Cornwall Railway was incorporated by Act of Parliament, with capital of £500,000 in £20 shares. Under the Act, the existing Hayle Railway was purchased by the new company, and was to be largely rebuilt and extended at either end to reach Truro and Penzance. Economic difficulties, both local and national, then

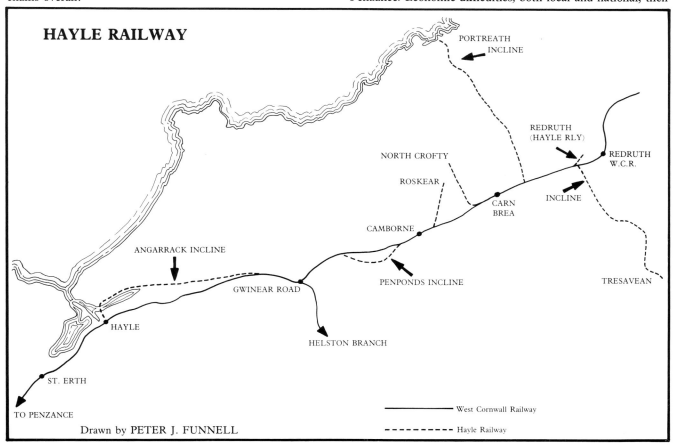

HAYLE RAILWAY

PORTREATH INCLINE

REDRUTH (HAYLE RLY)

REDRUTH W.C.R.

NORTH CROFTY

ROSKEAR

CARN BREA

INCLINE

CAMBORNE

ANGARRACK INCLINE

PENPONDS INCLINE

TRESAVEAN

GWINEAR ROAD

HAYLE

HELSTON BRANCH

ST. ERTH

TO PENZANCE

———————— West Cornwall Railway

- - - - - - - - - - Hayle Railway

Drawn by PETER J. FUNNELL

put a virtual halt on the proceedings, and it was not until 1850 that any progress was made in actual construction.

Work began that year on the Penzance section, albeit under new circumstances allowing the adoption of the standard gauge 4ft 8½in, and not broad gauge as originally specified. This was done for reasons of economy, but provision had to be made for the works to accommodate broad gauge traffic when it was eventually introduced. Brunel also recommended the use of Barlow rail on grounds of economy, 'both in first cost and in subsequent maintenance when compared with the cost of rails of equal strength'. It was also argued that with this rail, 'the alteration of gauge can be effected almost without expense, or at all events at so trifling a cost that it is not worth consideration.' From October 1851 the rails began to arrive, delivered by sea from Wales, and by 11th March 1852 the railway was able to open from Redruth to Penzance on a service of three trains daily in each direction.

On 25th August 1852 the official opening took place over the entire 25 mile route from Truro to Penzance. It was marked by a day of celebration, and a public holiday was declared at Penzance, where the town became the focus of attention. *The West Briton* recorded:

'Such numbers were never seen in the town before as assembled on this occasion to witness the demonstration and festivities . . . . The inhabitants showed their public spirit by uniting most heartily together, and the display they made to welcome the event was such as was never before produced in any other town in Cornwall.'

There were many enthusiastic travellers that day, with the greater part of the population of West Cornwall there to witness the occasion. Such was the traffic, that the special train bearing the Mayor, the Company Chairman Mr. H.O. Willis, directors and shareholders to Truro for a board meeting was well over an hour late when it eventually returned to Penzance. Their train was held in the crossing loop at Camborne to wait whilst three 'up' trains passed through. On arrival the train was welcomed by a gunners' salute along with other improvised greetings from both land and sea. There were, of course, the inevitable commemorative arches of evergreen decorated with flowers and banners. Town bands, speeches, dancing, suppers and fireworks added to the festive atmosphere, whilst representatives of the Company, together with invited guests, enjoyed a dinner to mark their achievement.

The arrival of the railway signified progress, which obviously meant change. This was, indeed, the substance of an address to the directors of the West Cornwall Company, read out in their honour by the town clerk. Their initiative marked:

'The first successful effort for breaking down the barrier which has for so long a time separated this county from the eastern parts of England, and the establishment of facilities (the wondrous results of modern science) for bringing the stranger to our beautiful scenery, and salubrious climate, as well as conveying the produce from our soil, our seas and our mines, to all parts of Britain.'

Services to and from Penzance in the first months consisted of three trains daily in each direction on weekdays, but no service was provided on Sundays. The departure times from Penzance and Truro were: 8.30 a.m., 12.00 noon and 5.00 p.m. arriving at Truro Road (sited at the west end of the now Higher Town Tunnel) at 10.15 a.m., 1.45 p.m., and 6.45 p.m. respectively. Departures from Truro were: 7.38 a.m., 2.00 p.m. and 7.00 p.m. arriving at Penzance at 9.20 a.m., 3.45 p.m., and 8.45 p.m., respectively. Accommodation was provided for first, second and third class on a journey time of 1¾ hours; the trains stopping at all stations. During October 1852 an extra 'up' train was introduced from Penzance to Redruth, departing at 10.00 a.m. arriving at Redruth at 11.05 a.m. Passengers could also reach Penryn and Falmouth by connecting omnibuses at Redruth, these meeting through services over the line in both directions.

Travel arrangements from Penzance to locations further afield were also developed. By taking the early morning departure from the town passengers could join the *Magnet* coach service from Truro to Plymouth, where, in turn, they could avail themselves of the Mail train for Exeter and Bristol. A corresponding service applied westward to Penzance. Excursion traffic also became well established on the 'West Cornwall' bringing useful revenue and some very interesting workings. Temperance

ST MICHAEL'S MOUNT

A Besley print of early railway working circa 1860. A train is pictured having just passed Marazion with St. Michaels Mount dominating the scene. The GWR produced many holiday posters featuring St. Michaels Mount as a great incentive to tourism.   *Courtesy of Cornwall County Museum, Truro*

A Besley print of the 1860s showing the original West Cornwall terminus in the context of the town generally. The extremely restricted passenger accommodation is evident here: note also the railings along the wall to protect the low station roof. These railings are still in position today, marking the site of the building prior to redevelopment in 1879. The goods shed and the line leading out onto Albert Pier are also shown clearly.

Redruth Local Studies Library

excursions and Sunday School outings were particularly popular and Penzance soon became a favourite destination.

Railway development also brought detailed changes to the landscape on the eastern side of the town. The two miles of single line running along the shoreline of Mounts Bay became a popular attraction for passengers, and a considerable bonus for GWR publicity in later years. Immediately before entering the station trains crossed the 347 yards of Penzance Viaduct, built of timber and in parts only 12 feet high. It stood in an extremely exposed position on the beach itself, and was to be the source of great concern on several occasions. The actual railway premises transformed their particular part of the town. They occupied, in part, the site of what had been private gardens, and gave the entire area a new perspective with the station building, cliff retaining wall and sea wall development.

Station facilities at Penzance were decidedly modest under the West Cornwall Railway and bore little or no resemblance to those provided by the Great Western from 1879. The station occupied a site on roughly the same position as the present building, but it did not extend as far westward towards the town as did its successor; nor was it remotely as spacious. It was a small wooden building with a low overall roof that barely reached the height of the retaining wall adjacent, and was always restricted particularly with the cliff wall and road to the north and the sea

on the south. When the broad gauge was extended to Penzance late in 1866 the difficulties were intensified. Goods facilities were also open to criticism on the grounds that the allotted covered provision was inadequate given the rapid growth of traffic.

Whilst the actual location of the railway had much to recommend it aesthetically, proximity to the sea, the shifting sands along the shore and the problems of flooding along the marshes east of Marazion, gave the company frequent cause for concern.

The viaduct was most vulnerable for the reasons outlined above, and not long after opening it was extensively damaged. On the night of 26th/27th December 1852 over 180 feet of timber work was swept away in a storm. Gales and spring tides combined and, unfortunately, the entire scaffolding and woodwork for the new south pier extensions at the harbour was demolished, and was carried ashore in the storm crashing against the viaduct. Together with the damage to the viaduct some 835 feet of the granite sea wall at the station was destroyed. Train services were terminated temporarily at Marazion whilst repairs were carried out. Again in 1856 a returning excursion carrying the Wesleyan Sunday School party was halted at its east end, because, 'the sea was so violently assaulting the viaduct'. The passengers left the train and walked the remaining distance to the station. This was but one isolated incident, but the most serious damage was to

THE VIADUCT OF THE PENZANCE RAILWAY, IN PART DESTROYED BY THE LATE GALE.

A contemporary print showing the damage done to Penzance Viaduct by extremely rough seas during a storm on the night of 26th/27th December 1852. Over 180 feet of timber work was swept away in this obviously exposed location just east of the station.

Cornwall County Museum

follow in January 1869 when it was demolished completely in dreadful storm conditions. The details will be considered later.

Marazion Road, renamed Marazion in October 1896, was a single platform station built on land reclaimed from the marsh. Originally the marshes reached down to the shore at this location and it was necessary to ensure adequate drainage to protect the line. Despite culverts, tunnels and outfall pipes that can still be seen today, flooding along the marsh always presented a threat.

The sea was not the only problem. From 1856 there were faults with the Barlow rail. The South Wales Railway had used the Barlow rail and found problems leading to its replacement, but in West Cornwall, where economy was the watchword, it could not be so easily removed. Careful maintenance, particularly in ballast work, brought improved stability and incidents of derailment and damage to stock were 'much diminished'. The gradual replacement of Barlow rail began in 1861, but it was a slow process. In the meantime, however, the Cornwall Railway, originally incorporated on the same day as the West Cornwall, completed its line from Plymouth, across the Tamar, to Truro. This brought a whole new perspective to railway interests in Cornwall, and bringing fundamental changes in the social and economic structure of the county. Penzance station became the gateway to the rest of the country for the people of the extreme south-west: it was also, of course, the gateway into the district for tourists.

The Main Line: Gwinear Road — Penzance

At this point it would seem appropriate to describe the main line route from the point of our survey at Gwinear Road to Penzance.

From Gwinear Road westward the line makes a continuous descent of 4¼ miles to the shores of the Hayle Estuary. At first this descent is relatively gentle averaging 1 in 176, but closeby milepost 316¾, ¾ mile from Gwinear Road, the gradient sharpens to 1 in 61 for a mile to Angarrack Viaduct. Milepost 316¾ also marks the point where the West Cornwall Railway of 1852 deviated south of the original alignment of the Hayle Railway (1837-1852). The latter pursued a straight course westward dropping down to sea level at Hayle via the 30 chain Angarrack Incline on a gradient of 1 in 10.

An inclined plane (there was another east of Gwinear Road at Penponds) was obviously unsatisfactory for the West Cornwall Company's line from Truro to Penzance, and could not be tolerated. Instead, their line descended on its somewhat winding course through two cuttings to Angarrack Viaduct just east of milepost 318. The viaduct was 266 yards long and 100 feet high. Originally of timber, with stone piers added, the entire structure was rebuilt in masonry and opened on 5th October 1885. Construction work brought its problems, however, with loss of life and labour disputes marking its history. The short lived Angarrack station on the north side of the line was at milepost 318. It opened in 1852 and closed the following year.

Just over ¼ mile beyond Angarrack was the original Guildford Viaduct; again, a timber structure with stone piers added. This viaduct, 128 yards long and 56 feet high, was rebuilt in masonry, opening on 5th October 1886. The line then passes south of the Copperhouse district of Hayle, running on an average gradient of 1 in 80 to Hayle station itself.

Since the opening of the West Cornwall Railway in 1852 Hayle has been the only permanent station between Gwinear Road and St Erth. Angarrack had its small station west of the viaduct at milepost 318, and from 1st July 1905 – 1st May 1908 Copperhouse Halt, between Angarrack and Hayle station served the community in that particular part of the town. It was a single platform on the south side of the line.

The GWR station at Hayle comprised 'up' and 'down' platforms, the line westward to St Erth being doubled in September 1899, and eastward to Angarrack in December 1909. A booking office, waiting room and main buildings were on the 'down' (south) side where there was also a goods shed and yard with siding access from the east. On the 'up' platform was a small waiting room and an extremely attractive signalbox, both towards the west end. The signalbox controlled movements over its paricular section of the main line and those on the Hayle Wharves branch. Behind the signalbox was a loop line, not served by the platform. Beyond this, again, was a water tank, a small single road locomotive shed and further sidings curving round at right angles to the main line, above the wharves branch.

Construction of the wharves branch gave valuable links with the quayside and the western end of the original Hayle Railway opened from December 1837. The branch curved away

Hayle signalbox on the 'up' platform. This controlled movements on and off the Wharves branch, this being its only effective purpose during the final years prior to demolition. It was somewhat similar in appearance to the signalbox at Dawlish in South Devon.

Lens of Sutton

northward from the west end of the station and fell sharply on a gradient of 1 in 30. It served, primarily, the wharves and gasworks at the northern end of the harbour area nearest the sea. Access along Penpol Quay to the site of the original Hayle Railway terminus beneath the viaduct was also possible. Shunting operations on this section of the line were carried out by horses until the beginning of the 1960s. Opening in 1852, the Wharves branch closed entirely in 1983. Mixed gauge working

Hayle looking westward in the 1920s. The goods shed can be seen on the 'down' side, whilst opposite is the signalbox, water tower and the small locomotive shed. Hayle viaduct is immediately beyond the west end of the station. *Local Studies Library, Redruth*

from October 1877 allowed access to broad gauge trains, until final conversion in 1892 of course.

Immediately west of the station was Hayle Viaduct. This was 277 yards long and 34 feet high, being rebuilt in October 1886. The viaduct crosses Foundry Square, and, at its east end, the former terminus of the Hayle Railway. The quayside is closeby to the north of the line showing ample evidence of Hayle's once considerable status as a trading port. A gentle descent through a cutting then leads out onto the shore of the Hayle Estuary, a magnificent location rich in wildlife, natural beauty and historical association. Curving along the shore the line then climbs a short but stiff gradient of 1 in 70 to St Erth, the junction for St Ives. This classic GWR station is described in detail in the section on the St Ives branch and needs no more comment here.

From St Erth the line continues to climb at 1 in 67 for almost ¾ mile then begins its descent to the south coast at Marazion, the steepest gradient being a short section at 1 in 86. Other than the slightest ripple immediately west of Marazion station the line follows a level course along the shores of Mounts Bay to the terminus itself. This final section of line has also been described extensively elsewhere in the text.

The entire 10¾ mile journey from Gwinear Road westward is extremely interesting from both an aesthetic and an historical point of view. It is also unique. Nowhere else in Britain can one cross the country from the north to south coasts in under ten minutes. This is but one example of the attraction and charm of this distinctive part of the country, rightly made famous by the GWR as the 'Cornish Riviera.'

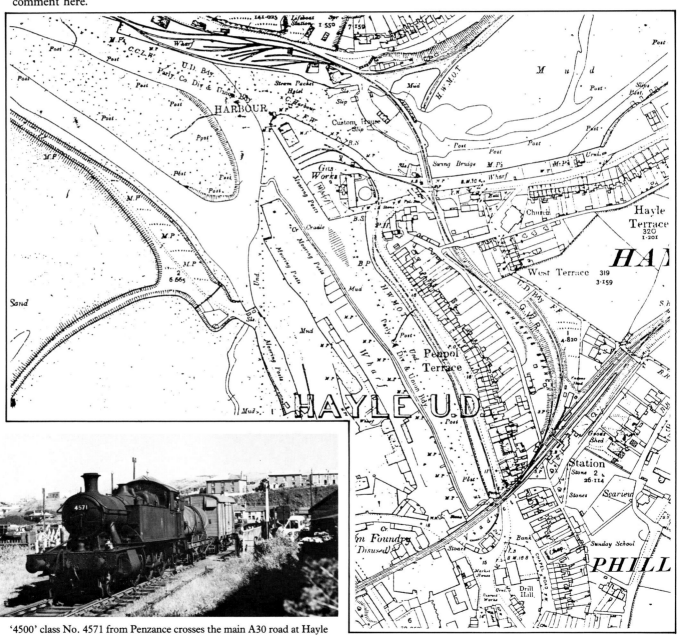

'4500' class No. 4571 from Penzance crosses the main A30 road at Hayle whilst working the Wharves branch in the summer of 1959. The branch enjoyed good business at this time with coal traffic, oil and chemicals.

P.Q. Treloar

Chapter Two
Through the Broad Gauge Years

The Royal Albert Bridge over the Tamar was officially opened by His Royal Highness Prince Albert on 2nd May 1859; services between Plymouth and Truro commencing two days later. There were celebrations at Penzance to mark the events. The town council proposed that tradespeople be invited to close their premises at 4 p.m. on 3 May and that a procession should be formed to meet the mayor and corporation from their train on arrival at 5.30 p.m. and conduct them to the Guildhall, thence to the Union Hotel for a public dinner. The civic leaders of the town had joined the celebrations at Truro witnessing the official opening from Plymouth westward to link with trains on the West Cornwall. Celebrations at Penzance were not as extensive as in 1852, but there was a real sense of achievement in gaining a continuous rail link with London despite the break of gauge.

One of the clearest expressions of change following this development was the notice published in the timetables for services from 11th May. (From that date West Cornwall trains to and from Truro concentrated on the new station following the opening of Higher Town Tunnel.) 'London Time is kept at all stations which is 22½ minutes faster than Penzance Time.' On the Cornwall line a similar notice was included: 'Greenwich Time is kept at all stations. It is 20 minutes earlier than Truro Time.' The Penzance town clock was then set to London time; a symbolic move, and a prerequisite for a working timetable.

Train services to and from Penzance under the new arrangements provided for five departures during weekdays, two on Sundays, and four arrivals, two on Sundays. Journeys beyond Truro involved changing to or from broad gauge trains. Penzance departures were as follows:

WEEKDAYS

6.15 a.m. arr. Truro 8.05 a.m. for Plymouth arr. 10.30 a.m. Paddington arr. 6.00 p.m.

8.55 a.m. arr. Truro 10.45 a.m. for Plymouth arr. 1.50 p.m. Bristol arr. 8.50 p.m.

1.45 p.m. arr. Truro 3.35 p.m. for Plymouth arr. 6.40 p.m. Paddington arr. 4.45 a.m.

4.35 p.m. Passengers and Goods arr. Truro 6.35 p.m. for Plymouth arr. 9.45 p.m.

7.44 p.m. arr. Truro 9.34 p.m. (Newham terminus, West Cornwall Railway).

SUNDAYS

9.09 a.m. arr. Truro 10.59 a.m. for Bristol dep. Truro 3.50 p.m. arr. 12.25 a.m.

7.05 p.m. arr. Truro 8.55 p.m.

PENZANCE ARRIVALS: WEEKDAYS

8.40 a.m. dep. Truro 6.50 a.m. (Newham terminus).

11.00 a.m. dep. Truro 9.10 a.m. from Plymouth 6.05 a.m. Paddington dep. 8.10 p.m.

3.37 p.m. dep. Truro 1.37 p.m. from Plymouth 10.10 a.m. Exeter dep. 6.55 a.m.

7.05 p.m. dep. Truro 5.15 p.m. from Plymouth 2.05 p.m. Bristol dep. 7.50 a.m.

SUNDAYS

11.00 a.m. dep. Truro 9.10 a.m. from Bristol dep. 12.40 a.m.

8.56 p.m. dep. Truro 7.06 p.m. from Bristol dep. 7.50 a.m.

Fares for the full journey from Penzance to Truro in May 1859 were listed as follows:—

First Class: Single 5/–   Second Class: Single 3/6
       Return 7/6   Return 5/8

Third Class: Single Ticket Only 2/2d.

Trains continued to serve all stations on the line and accommodation was provided for all three classes. From the latter half of 1862, however, third class travel was restricted to two trains daily.

From May 1859 traffic on the West Cornwall line certainly increased. With the new incentive for travel and trade, this far from prosperous company managed to pay modest dividends in good years such as 1862 and 1863. Perishable traffic – vegetables and fish – from the Penzance area and the promise of a growing tourist trade, helped enormously.

Now that the Cornwall Railway had reached Truro, however, it was incumbent upon their West Cornwall neighbour to observe the legal requirement of the 1850 Act: to lay broad gauge to Penzance. The estimated costs for the provision of this uniform gauge (quoted by *The West Briton* at £100,000) was a sum far in excess of anything available to the West Cornwall Company, and, in consequence, the Associated Companies, being the Great Western, Bristol and Exeter and South Devon railways, took effective possession of the line in an Act of 1865. Soon after the Act was passed, work began on the installation of the broad gauge, and from 6th November 1866 freight trains on the new gauge began working to and from Penzance. Passenger services followed four months later on 1st March 1867 marking a further decisive stage in railway development. For the next twenty-five years broad gauge working prevailed.

The first broad gauge working to Penzance on normal revenue earning service was the through goods from Falmouth on Tuesday 6th November 1866. The train comprised fifteen wagons and one brake-van, and was hauled by the South Devon locomotive *Atlas*. A considerable part of the train was taken with a large wheat consignment, landed at Falmouth, and bound for a local supplier in Penzance. Broad gauge passenger traffic was also expected to begin within a month, but in the event, it was held, pending the required clearances from the Board of Trade. Services did not then begin, until 1st March; fifteen years after the arrival of the first trains at Penzance.

With the new through services there was an overall improvement in journey times. The delay at Truro was now eliminated, and allowed later departure and earlier arrival times at Penzance. Arrivals and departures from Paddington remained unaltered. In January, for example the 9.15 a.m. train from Paddington gave an arrival time at Penzance of 9.05 p.m., in March the through coaches arrived ten minutes earlier at 8.55 p.m. Similarly, the January timing of the 6.15 a.m. departure from Penzance to connect for Paddington 6.15 p.m. was re-set to 6.23 a.m. The 'limited' night Mail trains took longer: 12½ hours from Penzance, and 13¼ hours from Paddington, but they also showed better performances by up to 25 minutes. Third class passengers could also travel from Paddington to Penzance within the day by leaving London at 6.00 a.m. and changing at Bristol to await the express; arriving Penzance 8.55 p.m.

Overall, there were five passenger trains each way on weekdays, and two on Sundays serving Penzance. All trains served every station over the West Cornwall line. Two of the weekday trains, in each direction, conveyed through coaches between Paddington and Penzance, and all services, with the exception of one local return working from Truro to Penzance, were broad gauge. For goods traffic, there was one through service daily on the broad gauge, but local trains were worked on the narrow gauge.

Lelant station on the St. Ives branch. This early photograph in broad gauge days shows a group of staff posing for the camera. Behind them is the attractive wooden station house with the Hayle Estuary to the right.

Cornwall County Museum

The provision of a mixed goods working between Truro and Penzance in November 1871, however, marked one of the most unusual practices to be found on the railway system of Britain at the time, although the Windsor branch had also run mixed gauge passenger trains on some services. Narrow gauge wagons were worked with those of the broad gauge by means of a match-truck, specially fitted with large buffers and adjustable couplings. Its function was to link the two very different types of rolling stock, thereby incorporating them into a working unit. Motive power for these trains was provided by narrow gauge locomotives. The mixed gauge workings improved the flow of through goods wagons to and from Penzance and these unusual trains were retained until the end of the broad gauge in 1892.

Passenger services were also improved in 1871. During June the down 'Mail' was accelerated by 1¼ hours to arrive at Penzance at 8.10 a.m. whilst the 'up' train departed later in the afternoon, at 3.50 p.m., making a difference of 45 minutes. Passengers from Paddington, other than third class, could now also benefit from a later day-time departure for Penzance. The 11.45 a.m. *Flying Dutchman* was extended from Plymouth to Penzance with an arrival time of 10.04 a.m. '326 miles in ten hours and nineteen minutes – an unquestionable improvement and an immense boon to persons in business.' Such was the verdict of *The West Briton*. Another useful service for both business and leisure purposes was the new early morning train from Plymouth to Penzance, at 6.55 a.m. This replaced the 8.10 departure and, stopping at all stations, it allowed for a comfortable round trip to the far west of Cornwall within the day. The narrow gauge stopping train was discontinued during 1871.

From June 1879, the Great Western introduced a new express service that cut the journey time to Paddington considerably. The new train was booked to depart from Penzance at 11.15 a.m. making limited stops to Plymouth North Road (2.15 p.m.) thence calling at Mutley, Newton Abbot, Teignmouth, Exeter, Taunton, Bristol, Bath and Swindon; arriving at Paddington at 8.10 p.m. The overall journey time was 8 hours 55 minutes, as compared with the previous best of 10 hours 20 minutes. The corresponding service from Paddington, departing 9.00 a.m., terminated at Plymouth after a six hour run. Passengers from Paddington to Penzance had to travel on the *Flying Dutchman* departing from the capital at 11.45 a.m. From Plymouth, however, the *Dutchman* was accelerated considerably, making only ten stops as against a previous twenty-two: the new arrival time at Penzance was 9.05 p.m. gaining an hour overall. Third class passengers, however, faced a total journey of 11 hours 50 minutes from Paddington to Penzance by leaving London at 9.00 a.m.

During the final decade leading to the end of the broad gauge there were further important accelerations. From 1884 the night mail trains were no longer of limited accommodation. Journey times in both directions were improved: from Paddington the timing was 10 hours 35 minutes, departing at 9 p.m.; from Penzance the timing was 11 hours with a late departure, moved from 3.50 p.m. to 5.00 p.m. The provision of third class accommodation was of particular significance.

Detailed improvements were also made to working arrangements at the terminus once broad gauge services began. A great deal of important work was carried out during the 1870s in

An overall view of the railway looking east along the shore of Mounts Bay, circa 1880. The exposed position of the viaduct is more than apparent here. Note the broad gauge goods train having just passed the siding at Ponsandane (Gulval). The land to the left of the locomotive was seriously considered as the site for a new terminus during 1871 when the Associated Companies met with difficulties in developing the terminus itself. As traffic increased, the land to the south of the road was extensively developed by the GWR for sidings and their locomotive depot.

Courtesy of Cornwall County Museum, Truro

particular. This included the extension and overhaul of station facilities, the building of siding accommodation at Ponsandane, and the renewal of the viaduct over the beach. The problems with the viaduct took priority following the events of Sunday 31st January 1869.

Since opening in 1852 the viaduct had been subject to considerable damage from the sea. Each winter it was necessary to close it to traffic during the worst of the weather, but early in 1869 it was finally destroyed. *The West Briton* gave a graphic account of the event, beginning its report on the situation as it stood on the evening of Saturday 30 January.

'At 6.40 a.m. on Sunday morning as the 'up' train was ready to leave the station the guard stopped her before they ventured onto the viaduct and as it turned out they were fortunate that they proceeded no further. By 7 a.m. the viaduct began to show signs of weakness from the violence of the waves as the tide was at its height and an immense body of water was beating against the timbers. In fifteen minutes it began to give way and by 7.30 a.m. the greater half of it nearer Penzance was completely washed away. The train had to be detained and Mr. Denbigh and Mr. Bone at once proceeded to Marazion to communicate with the telegraph offices up the line requesting them to send engines and carriages, and to caution the 'down' mail. The telegraph wires were all carried away at Penzance. The sand and shingle covered the railway from Penzance to Marazion, and was, in some places, two to three feet deep. The marsh at Marazion flowed over the railway and between the sleepers and the ballast was washed away. It was doubtful for some time whether the train could safely venture across. A man was sent over the line to see if the sleepers were safe, whilst Messrs Denbigh and Bone found out the depth of water on each side of the line, and they thought that

the engine might venture and the train was at length safely brought over to Marazion station. Omnibuses ran to Penzance from this point and the mails and passengers were forwarded to Penzance.'

As a result of similar weather conditions in South Devon, the seawall at Dawlish was also breached, flooded and closed to traffic. At Penzance a temporary arrangement was organised whereby the line was moved a little way inland of the viaduct on land given by the Bolitho family. Nevertheless, there was serious disruption to traffic and the Associated Companies expressed particular concern over the probable damage to traffic in broccoli and fish.

On 1st November 1871 a new viaduct opened to traffic. It was three feet higher than the original, with granite piers at the western end, where it crossed the river, and bolted timbers elsewhere. The entire structure was 1050 feet long, and cost in excess of £3,000 to build; it took six months to complete and carried a single line. Permission to build the viaduct was granted only upon the final decision of an inquiry by a Select Committee of the House of Commons which reported in April 1871. This enquiry also addressed itself to the two other current controversial issues: the extension of the station and the construction of sidings at Ponsandane.

On 28th September 1869, the railway companies had made formal application to Penzance Town Council and the Bolitho family, as landowners, for permission to modernise and extend the station complex southward towards Albert Pier and the sea. It was emphasised that the existing arrangements were overcrowded and inadequate, but despite support from the Bolitho family, the Town Council expressed opposition to railway development. The railway declined the terms offered them by the council and following the latter's rejection of a further bill to enlarge the site in February 1871, the Associated Companies adopted a new approach.

In March instructed surveyors, acting on behalf of the companies, were to begin work on plans for an entirely new terminal complex outside the town on land at Ponsandane. An interesting feature of these proposals was the location of the new site on the north side of the main road (now the A30) which would have radically altered the pattern of railway development at Penzance. These plans would require the construction of a bridge to carry the road over the railway, whilst the site itself, immediately to the east of the Gulval river, was ideal for unhindered expansion. It was open, flat, land that, when drained, would have freed the railway completely of the restriction of the cliff wall and the sea. Moreover, it would remove the problems linked with the viaduct approach to the town. Within a week of the survey work beginning, however, the council appeared to take a more conciliatory approach, apparently seeing the new plans as more controversial than the original proposals. The debate on station development also became involved with other plans to build siding accommodation at Ponsandane. The latter also came in for considerable opposition.

In March 1870 the Associated Companies stated their intention to build a goods siding between the Gulval river (Ponsandane) and Long Rock. It was stated at the time that a siding at this location would provide the necessary facility for the considerable traffic in broccoli and potatoes from the Gulval area together with the large consignments of corn arriving from Falmouth. The town council considered the plan an encroachment, and this question also was referred to the inquiry.

The Select Committee announced its findings on all three subjects, on 3rd April 1871. Concerning the viaduct, it had stipulated that the original line be constructed on its former site; in regard to the siding it was very specific. Permission to build was granted, but with the provision that 'no rails shall come within fifty feet of the road; and that no building shall be erected therein of a height greater than twelve feet from the level of the rails to the top of the roof'. The 'splendid views' from the Bolitho estate, situated to the north of the line, were to be protected by means of this latter stipulation. In addition, a specially sited grass bank was raised in front of the sidings to hide them from view at the estate. The signal box at Ponsandane, built after the turn of the century, was also required to be fitted with a flat roof for the same reason. Construction work on the siding followed accordingly, and future development for the original station was also approved. All plans to build a new station complex at Ponsandane were dropped.

The 1870s were crucially important to the railways of West Cornwall. The biggest single event being in February 1876, when the GWR assumed control of the entire system west of Bristol. Soon after, in April 1878, work began on a new terminus at Penzance. The 4¼ mile branch line to St. Ives opened on 1st June 1877. (Work on a new junction station at St. Erth had already started by 1874). Marazion station was also rebuilt from 1879 on a more ambitious scale. Earlier, in 1871, the railway companies had drawn up plans for improvements at Penzance, including the demolition of fourteen dwelling houses along the cliff road, east of the station. This was done to develop the site as a new locomotive depot, but it did not open until 1876.

Looking to the closing years of the nineteenth century, an entire era of Great Western Railway history came to a swift and deliberate end during one weekend in May 1892. The company had decided upon the elimination of broad gauge to standardise working practice across the system. Penzance participated directly in the final hours of broad gauge activity.

The last train from Paddington to Penzance, *The Cornishman*, left London at 10.15 a.m. on Friday 20th May. All along the route large numbers of people turned out to witness its passing, whilst on board, there were noteworthy personalities including Henry Lambert, General Manager GWR, and Colonel Edgecombe, Company Director. At Penzance a large gathering welcomed the train, booked on this occasion to arrive at 8.20 p.m. Many people at Penzance bought return tickets to Marazion on the 8.05 train in order to enjoy a last journey back over the broad gauge on *The Cornishman*. Inspector Harris also travelled out on the 8.05 service, but his destination was St. Ives, in order to ensure that the branch was cleared of broad gauge stock and to issue the appropriate certificate. The last broad gauge service on the branch was the 8.25 p.m. departure from St. Erth arriving St. Ives at 8.40 p.m. This train returned empty stock from St. Ives at 8.50 p.m. with Inspector Harris.

Two empty stock trains left Penzance and St. Erth at 7.05 p.m. and 9.15 p.m. respectively, but the final working was to leave Penzance at 9.45 p.m. Inspector Scantlebury issued the official certificate to the stationmaster and signalmen at the terminus notifying clearance and the last broad gauge train left Penzance for Swindon. Two locomotives, six coaches and a breakdown van from Newton Abbot comprised this auspicious working; the engineering staff then took possession of the line, and the broad gauge passed into history. On the following Monday morning passenger services commenced on the narrow gauge; the coaching stock for Penzance and St. Ives having been previously worked down on broad gauge wagons and stored at Gwinear Road and Helston in preparation. The GWR then entered upon a new era.

Timetable for July, August and September 1883

Departures from Penzance			Arrivals at Penzance		
Weekdays	**Arrive**		**Weekdays**		**Depart**
6.25 Paddington	6.00 p.m.		8.10	Paddington	8.10 p.m.
10.00 Paddington	10.20 p.m.		10.45	Plymouth	6.50 a.m.
11.15 Paddington	8.10 p.m.		12.45	Plymouth	8.50 a.m.
1.30 Exeter	9.15 p.m.		2.53	Bristol	6.15 a.m.
3.50 Paddington	4.35 a.m.		6.30	Paddington	5.30 a.m.
6.35 Plymouth	10.26 p.m.		8.50	Paddington	9.00 a.m.
			9.05	Paddington	11.45 a.m.
Sundays			**Sundays**		
8.20 Paddington	10.45 p.m.		8.10	Paddington	8.10 p.m.
3.50 Paddington	4.35 a.m.		6.28	Bristol	6.30 a.m.

Chapter Three
The Decades of Expansion

One of the first notable improvements after the gauge conversion was the introduction of corridor trains in June 1893. These first appeared on a Paddington – Birkenhead run in October 1892, and on 1st June the following year, they were incorporated into West of England services. The 10.15 a.m. from Paddington and the 10.45 a.m. from Penzance were formed with four coupled corridor coaches, together with a fifth, serving Falmouth, but not with connecting access. *The West Briton* considered it 'one of the greatest boons to the people of Cornwall that has been introduced by the GWR'. Gas lighting and steam heating were also emphasised as important in setting new standards of comfort and convenience.

The pursuit of higher standards of service was also reflected in the new schedule for *The Cornishman* introduced in July 1901. From the beginning of the month Penzance was reached in 7 hours 52 minutes, on a non-stop journey to Exeter, arriving in 3 hours 38 minutes, and a 5 hour run to Plymouth. Connecting services for the Cornish branch lines were emphasised in order to make this train a showpiece for the West Country. A corresponding service eastward departed from Penzance at 11 a.m. with an arrival time at Paddington of 7 p.m. Stops were made at St. Erth, Truro, Par, Plymouth, Exeter and Bristol. The mayor and corporation attended the departure of the inaugural run from Penzance. *The Cornishman* had set something of a precedent with its fast timings of 1896, and a new regular schedule was extremely valuable. This train has been widely recognised as a fore-runner to the *Cornish Riviera Express*, but it was also impor-

tant in that it offered new opportunities to develop traffic northward, via the Severn Tunnel. At Bristol the 'up' train connected with the 5 p.m. service to Shrewsbury, Crewe, Liverpool and Manchester, and was worked in conjunction with the LNWR. Similar facilities were extended to perishable traffic working this route.

Shortly after the turn of the century two new trains were introduced between Paddington and Penzance. The first, in January 1902, was the exclusive Postal Train; the TPO still runs today, maintaining its special mail status. The other, beginning on 1st July 1904, was *The Cornish Riviera Express* (but without its title at that time).

Prior to the new express entering service, officially, a trial or demonstration run was made to Penzance, on the previous day. It departed Paddington at 10.10 a.m. and reached Penzance at 4.57 p.m. thirteen minutes ahead of schedule. Mr. J.C. Inglis, General Manager, the traffic and carriage superintendants, and the divisional superintendant, West Cornwall, were amongst those on board the train, which also included members of the press. A celebratory dinner was held at The Queens Hotel that evening, and at 10.00 a.m. on the Friday morning, *City of Bath* drew its six-coach train out of the station to the strains of a military band assembled on the platform.

The pre-war services reached their peak with the introduction of *The Cornish Riviera Express*. This train was made up of five coaches and a dining car for Penzance, and a through coach serving Falmouth. A seven hour run was made between

The 'up' *Cornish Riviera Express* leaving Penzance at 10.00 a.m. headed by 'Bulldog' class 4-4-0 No. 3450 *Swansea*. It is seen here at the eastern end of the viaduct, running over the beach itself. The *Cornish Rivera Express* called at St Erth, Gwinear Road, Truro and Plymouth, whilst the 'down' service included an extra stop at Devonport.   *Courtesy of Cornwall County Museum, Truro*

Picking up the Mail at Long Rock. A curved framed 4-4-0 heads along the seashore at a spot now forming the western entrance to the HST depot. An exclusive TPO service between Paddington and Penzance was introduced in January 1902. This train was possibly the later afternoon departure also offering sleeper accommodation to Paddington.

Courtesy of Cornwall County Museum, Truro

TIMETABLE: JANUARY — APRIL, 1902

Penzance Arrivals

7.30 a.m.	Paddington dep. 10.00 p.m. Corridor Train — 1st, 2nd, 3rd classes.
9.13 a.m.	Truro dep. 8.00 — Stopping service.
11.02 a.m.	Paddington dep. 12.00 Midnight. Sleeping car Service (1st class) to Plymouth (via Millbay).
1.00 p.m.	Plymouth Mutley/North Road. dep. 9.08 (via Millbay).
2.47 p.m.	Bristol dep. 6.15 a.m. (via Millbay).
4.58 p.m.	Paddington dep. 5.30 a.m. (via Millbay).
7.10 p.m.	Paddington dep. 10.40 a.m. Penzance Corridor Express Luncheon car First Class.
8.41 p.m.	Plymouth Millbay dep. 4.55 Stopping service.
9.23 p.m.	Paddington dep. 11.45 a.m. Corridor Express (via Millbay).

Penzance Departures

6.15 a.m.	Truro arr. 7.22 (Mondays only) Stopping service.
7.55 a.m.	Paddington arr. 6.30 p.m. Plymouth/Exeter Corridor Express.
10.05 a.m.	Truro arr. 11.15 — Stopping service.
10.25 a.m.	Paddington arr. 7.00 p.m. 'Corridor Express'.
12.00 NOON	Paddington arr. 10.10 p.m. Stopping Train (Cornwall) thence 'Plymouth Express'.
1.48 p.m.	Plymouth Millbay arr. 5.35 p.m. Stopping service.
4.50 p.m.	Paddington arr. 4.05 a.m. Corridor Train with sleeping car Service from Plymouth. Sleeping cars remain at the platform in Paddington until 8.00 a.m. for passengers convenience.
6.40 p.m.	Plymouth Millbay arr. 10.22 p.m. Stopping service.
8.10 p.m.	Truro arr. 9.28 Stopping service.

Corridor Trains included reserved compartments for ladies, smoking saloons and lavatory compartments. Corridor services for Cornwall began in June 1893, with the 10.15 a.m. from Paddington and the 10.45 a.m. from Penzance. Falmouth was also served.

Paddington and Penzance, departing at 10.10 a.m. and 10.00 a.m. respectively, providing a service that was 'limited' in the most prestigious sense in terms of accommodation, of seat reservations at one shilling each, of service including a five course lunch at 2/6d, and selected stations served. The stops listed for the 'down' train for example were: Plymouth, Truro, Gwinear Road, St. Erth and Penzance. The 'up' train also called at Devonport.

From the summer of 1906 the journey was faster again, because the new direct route to and from Paddington via Westbury had opened. It was a reduction of almost twenty miles and the timings were cut back, first to 6 hours 40 minutes, then to 6 hours 35 minutes for the 'down' 10.30 a.m. The seven-coach sets of newly built Dreadnought stock, so called on account of their overall size, – 70 ft long and 9ft 6in wide – marked new developments. End and centre doors and an elliptical roof were new features departing from the clerestory style. Indeed, on the eve of World War One, the *Official Guide to Penzance* included the following statement in praise of the railway:

'Thanks to the enterprise of the Great Western Company . . . . (the journey to London) occupies only a few hours and nothing that can contribute to the travelling comfort and convenience is left undone. The Paddington to Penzance Expresses which make the longest non-stop run in England are among the fastest, the smoothest-running and most luxuriously appointed trains in the world'.

At Marazion, siding accommodation and the yard, north of the line, were developed. East of the station, the Company bought land to build sidings along the marsh, parallel and to the north of the main line. There was also a deviation for the road from Penzance to Marazion, where, west of the level crossing, it was re-aligned slightly northward. The yard was then extended considerably. Originally, it comprised a single siding and goods platform with two cranes and a loop running to the north of the station itself. In 1892 a new approach road for the enlarged yard was opened at the eastern end of Long Rock village and a lengthy goods platform 40 feet wide and approximately 800 feet long was constructed. The siding accommodation was transformed; five roads being available from the development. One particular siding reached, through a loop off the main line extended to a point over a quarter of a mile westward alongside the main line, close to the occupation crossing at Long Rock.

The station at Marazion had also been rebuilt for the 1880s by the contractor responsible for the new terminus at Penzance from 1878 – 1880: Messrs Vernon and Ewens of Cheltenham. Marazion gained a station far superior to the single platform arrangement of West Cornwall days. There were two platforms with main buildings of dressed granite, comprising: stationmaster's office, booking and parcels offices, waiting room, footbridge and signal box, on the 'down' side. A waiting room was also provided on the 'up' platform and sidings extended to the south of

The rebuilt Marazion station viewed from the west end of the 'down' platform early this century. With very few alterations, it retained this appearance generaly until closure in October 1964. Note the covered footbridge similar to the one still in use at St Erth. The smoke stains on the overbridge, carrying the Penzance Helston road, are on the 'down' side only indicating that single track was still in use between Marazion and St Erth until 1929.
Local Studies Library, Redruth

Detailed plans for development at Ponsandane, Long Rock and Marazion were drawn up in 1892 to give extra siding accommodation. Land to the west of Long Rock level crossing (today's automatic barrier) was purchased by the Company thereby securing the site to be later occupied by the locomotive depot. Further west, the siding accommodation at Ponsandane, first developed in 1871, was extended to give more lines and platform space. One siding was built westward, from Ponsandane, parallel to the main line on its north side, terminating at the Gulval river.

the site close to the stationmaster's house. A goods loop was also carried to the rear of the 'up' platform, but the projected sidings along the marsh to the east were not built.

Further improvements followed on 16th August 1893 with the doubling of the line from Marazion station to Ponsandane. This was protected from storm damage by a sea wall built on the section from Marazion to Long Rock, where the line ran close to the high water mark. Long Rock and Ponsandane signal boxes were opened following these developments along the shore.

'Bulldog' 4-4-0 *Penzance* poses along with the locomotive shed staff outside the original loco depot at Chyandour, immediately east of Penzance station itself. The depot was built in 1876 and was replaced in 1914 by the Churchward-designed accommodation further eastward at Long Rock. This photograph dates from the period immediately prior to World War One, circa 1909/1910.

Cornwall County Museum

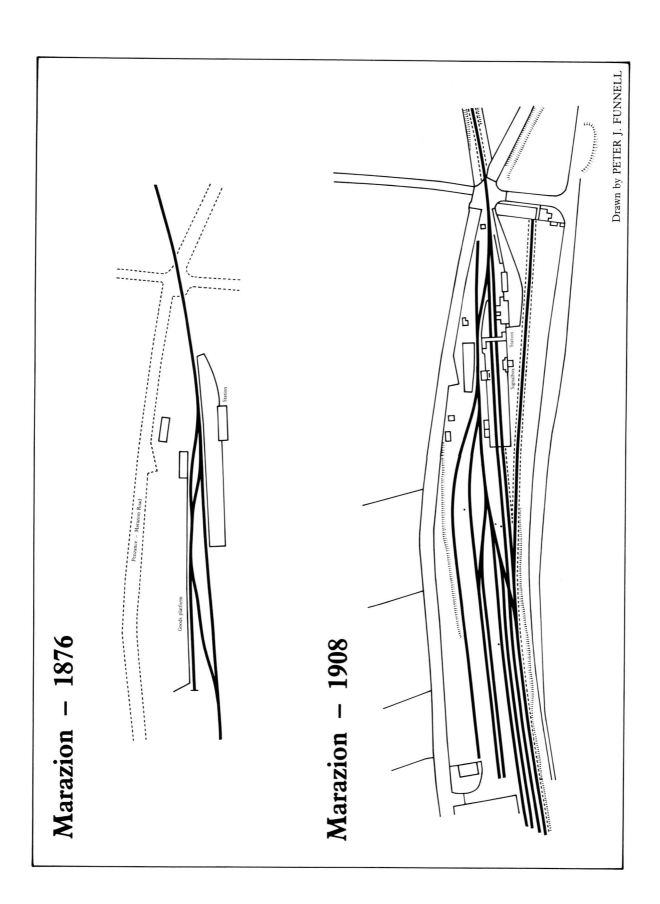

Marazion – 1876

Marazion – 1908

Drawn by PETER J. FUNNELL

This photograph shows the demolition gang at work on Penzance viaduct. The viaduct was replaced in 1921 by a stone embankment carrying double track for the main line and provision for sidings.

Cornwall County Museum

Ponsandane signalbox. When built in the early years of this century it was necessary to fit a flat roof as shown here. This was required because the Bolitho family, important local landowners, would not tolerate unrestricted growth of the railway along the shoreline. The flat roof ensured that the view of Mounts Bay from the windows of Chyandour House was unspoiled, and that the railway, as far as possible, was kept out of sight! *Author*

Long Rock signalbox, further eastward, controlled all movements to and from the locomotive sheds. Like Ponsandane, this box was literally built on the beach and its rear wall was within reach of the strong spring tides. *Author*

Two troublesome level crossings further eastward were also removed on plans drawn for 1892. These were at Rosevidney, between Marazion and St. Erth, and at St. Erth itself. Both were replaced by bridges, requiring road traffic to follow a minor deviation, but the line between St. Erth and Marazion was not doubled until 16th June 1929.

The next major development to affect working arrangements at Penzance was the opening of a new locomotive depot on the land gained immediately west of Long Rock.

This new depot was opened in 1914 and was a standard example of the Churchward 'Straight Shed' design. It comprised a four-road shed with workshops, coaling stage, turntable and pumping and boiler houses, making a vast improvement on the restricted conditions experienced at the old depot. The latter was a two-road construction with a coaling shed, water-tower and turntable dating from 1876. It occupied a site immediately east of the station on land claimed by the demolition of twenty dwelling houses and a yard area owned by the Bolitho family. The new shed at Long Rock, however, must have been the best placed depot, aesthetically, in Britain, with St. Michaels Mount and the sea as a backdrop. A modern depot clearly reflected the progressive image of the GWR confirming the Company's commitment to the future.

The railway dominated the local economy during the inter-war years, and important new working patterns emerged. Tourism, market gardening and dairying, collectively, had an enormous impact and were all dependent upon the Great Western.

Soon after World War One the GWR began improving the immediate approaches to the terminus. The viaduct along the shore was replaced with a substantial stone embankment of far greater strength and proportions that allowed for additional track improvements. This work together with the removal of the old locomotive depot, close by, was a permanent solution improving the character of the station considerably.

The granite embankment ran for a quarter of a mile along the shoreline, curving in a south-westerly direction to the station. There was a bridged section at the western end to cross the Coombe river whilst, to the east, the embankment merged with the sand dunes above the shore. The entire structure was protected from the sea by large numbers of cut granite boulders piled along the shoreline to take the full impact of the waves in storm conditions. The stonework was delivered in special consignments from quarries at Princetown and Penryn.

The embankment was opened to traffic on 24th July 1921; carrying a double-track main line and a siding, to the north, on a loop. This siding, known locally as 'the slopers' was extremely useful for storing empty coaching stock, close by the station, and extended from a point immediately west of Ponsandane signal box to the terminus itself.

This work improved operating conditions considerably. The line itself was well protected, guaranteeing continuous movement of traffic during winter, and double track was now installed over the entire route along the shore to Marazion.

Further detailed improvements along the shoreline came in 1935/36, when sidings at Ponsandane and Marazion were extended in response to increased traffic, especially in perishables. Goods platforms at Ponsandane were also extended to allow four trains to be loaded or serviced, and extra accommodation for empty coaching stock was provided. Land to the east of the station at Marazion was taken to construct four lines of sidings, two on each side of the main line, along the marsh.

Marazion had also seen important developments in June 1929, when the line was doubled from the station, eastward to St. Erth. Prior to this, the entire east end of the station was remodelled. The platforms were lengthened and the level crossings removed in favour of a new road bridge over the railway. This called for a deviation for road traffic to and from Penzance and Hayle directions to lift it over the line. The original alignment, descending to the site of the former level crossing, then became the approach road to the station.

The two most significant projects initiated by the GWR during the inter-war years were the building of a new goods shed at Ponsandane and the development and modernisation of Penzance station. In both cases they were schemes to reflect the pre-eminent position of the Great Western in the local economy. Development of the station will be considered separately elsewhere, but at this stage it is useful to record that progress was well advanced by the winter of 1937.

New premises for freight traffic opened on 1st December 1937. In February that year, the local newspaper reported:

'In the course of time the complaints that have been made of inadequate accommodation at both passenger and goods stations will be remedied . . . . . Constructional development which will entirely transform the eastern entrance to Penzance is well under way at the GWR station and at Ponsandane. This building will take the goods traffic at present dealt with at the rear of the station at Penzance: the Penzance shed will be demolished as soon as the alternative is suitably advanced'.

The main building was 280 feet long and 40 feet wide, including an interior platform space, 30 feet wide, with special berthing for fourteen wagons at a time. Overhead craneways

Marazion looking to the west. The large goods yard can be seen here on the 'up' side. As it is obviously full with passenger coaches and parcel vans it is more than likely a weekend in summer when all siding space was at a premium.   *Lens of Sutton*

Above: The full extent of GWR development along the shores of Mounts Bay can be seen in these post nationalisation views. No. 6875 *Hindford Grange* heads eastward alongside the locomotive shed in October 1959. The GWR goods shed opened on 1st December 1937 can also be seen in the left background. The train is passing what is now the site of the HST depot.   *M. Mensing*

Left: The turntable with No. 6845 *Paviland Grange* about to proceed to the coaling stage. Note the sand and coal wagons for the depot on the right of the photograph. *P.Q. Treloar*

Below: The four-road locomotive shed at Long Rock opened in 1914. 'Castle' class No. 5048 *Earl of Devon* partly obscures the workshops and boiler house beyond, whilst two double-chimneyed 'Counties' one being No. 1011 *County of Chester*, stand either side of No. 6855 *Saighton Grange*. The two roads to the left of the photograph fell into disrepair once steam working ended in September 1962: the two remaining roads being adapted as the diesel shed. 9th September 1959.
P.Q. Treloar

were installed for easy movement and a glazed roof on the north side ensured good lighting. A verandah, 15 feet wide, also ran along the north side for protection from the weather when loading/unloading vehicles. A twenty ton weighbridge was installed at the entrance to the yard for animal traffic, farm produce and coal. Office accommodation was noteworthy for its standard of fittings, including central heating, high varnished woodwork and parc-ray style flooring.

The depot, embodied the high standards of service associated with the GWR and underlined its positive image locally. This was especially so in one respect. From the opening day, the company carried out all its deliveries to and from the depot by motor transport; lorries replaced the remaining horse-drawn vehicles which, in turn, made it possible to serve a much wider area efficiently.

Freight traffic more than justified the new investment, particularly in the latter half of the 1930s when government involvement in the economy stimulated agriculture locally.

Valuable improvements in freight transit were introduced in 1927. The 9.23 a.m. Old Oak Common – Penzance goods, vacuum braked and fitted with oil axle boxes, formed part of the new service, whereby non stop running between Newton Abbot and Liskeard was adopted. From Penzance, the 2.50 p.m. Bristol to Penzance goods worked on a limited loading principle, where wagons were not to exceed five tons working weight. Non-stop schedules were also provided between Newton Abbot and Liskeard on this fast fitted train. Other examples of fast services at this time included the 4.58 p.m. Marazion – Bristol and the 7.20 p.m. Penzance – Plymouth. Milk traffic was also improved, significantly, in 1927, when new 3,000 gallon milk tanks were introduced into the district. Prior to this, the movement of milk was by churns conveyed in Siphon 'C' and 'G' ventilated vans.

The introduction of these new services pre-dated the onset in 1929 of the worst period of economic depression yet experienced. From late 1921 until 1940 there were never less than a million people unemployed and the performance of the GWR must be seen in this sobering context. By 1934 prospects were better and opportunities for traffic improved, to the extent, that by 1939 the company had made significant progress in West Cornwall. This was more than apparent in the growth of freight traffic, whilst progress in passenger service was also an outstanding achievement.

From the turn of the century the GWR began to campaign to promote the West Country as the premier holiday region in Britain. After the dislocation of the war years which, surprisingly, at first did not result in any great changes to West Country services, the company began to build up its traffic. From 1st January 1917 to May 1919, journey times were lengthened and services cut back. The Cornish Riviera ceased to be a 'limited' working during this particular period, but by October 1921 it was restored to its pre-war schedule. Indeed, the prospects for development on the 'Holiday Line' to the west were, increasingly, set in sharp contrast to the gloomy forecasts for coal traffic in South Wales.

Acceleration of services followed in 1927 and again in 1929. In July 1929 The Cornish Riviera was timed to reach Penzance in 6 hours 20 minutes: ten minutes faster than the run from Paddington two years earlier. It also included through coaches for St. Ives. Extra Saturday trains from Paddington at 10.55 a.m. and Birmingham at 9.45 a.m., together with a weekday 11.05 a.m. departure from Paddington were also provided. The sleeper service to Paddington was given a later departure at 9.05 p.m. and not 8.35 p.m. as previously, and in the new winter timetables that year, third class sleeping cars were introduced to and from

Penzance. Sleeping berths were available at 6/- each. Locally, the summer timetable also provided four through workings from Penzance to St. Ives each weekday in view of the growing popularity of the resort.

The same year also saw the GWR bus services join the Western National Company. Registered as the Western National Omnibus Company Ltd. the new enterprise recorded at the time that road services were to be organised in conjunction with those of the railway on a policy of positive co-operation, not competition. The new company served South Devon, the district west of Exeter, and Cornwall.

The GWR's centenary celebration in 1935 provided the perfect opportunity to review progress and achievement to date. Holiday Haunts that year carried a specific feature entitled 'The Centenary of the Holiday Line.'

'Cornwall's development was bound up with many difficulties and is a story of huge expenditure in doubling railway lines that were single tracks, replacing an immense number of timber viaducts by granite and throwing out railway tentacles supplemented by motor services to resorts which one seemed inaccessible to Britain's millions. Now the names of Cornish coves are household words, but happily railway and local interests alike have resisted any temptation to convert enchanting beauty spots to busy centres, preferring to concentrate on the now famous towns while leaving the haunts of peace and beauty in all their natural loveliness'.

The Company also marked the occasion by showing its interest in the future.

New coaching stock was introduced that year for The Cornish Riviera service. The Centenary stock, as it was called, was built specifically for the Cornish Riviera Limited as it was now known, and embodied new standards of comfort and consideration for passengers. These coaches were 60 feet long and 9 feet 7 ins wide; dimensions that took every advantage of the former broad gauge loading limits, exclusive to the GWR. On weekdays the first stop, other than to change locomotives at Devonport, was Truro; whilst on Saturdays the train served only Penzance and St. Ives. The 'up' service ran on a corresponding schedule.

A new service, The Cornishman, was also introduced for the centenary year. This train maintained the impressive standards set by its earlier namesake at the turn of the century; the 'down' train leaving Paddington at 10.35 a.m. and the 'up' service starting from St. Erth at 10.20 a.m. The unusual practice of starting an important train from St. Erth was, however, something of an expedient, pending improvements at the terminus itself.

The 'down' Cornishman carried passengers for Weymouth and Plymouth, Newquay, Truro, Helston, St. Ives and Penzance, arriving at 5.07 p.m.; on the 'up' train, stops were made at Gwinear Road, Truro, Par and Plymouth, arriving at Paddington at 4.50 p.m. These schedules gave overall timings of 6 hours 32 minutes (down) and 6 hours 30 minutes for the slightly shorter journey from St. Erth, thereby, providing West Cornwall with a valuable new express service. The local newspaper commented favourably: 'The service this summer is the finest ever offered to the travelling public and is a sincere effort to cater for every type of passenger: holiday maker, businessman, housewife and scholar'.

Excursion traffic for 1935 was both varied and enterprising. Other than strictly local services, such as trips to Penzance from stations west of Truro for the annual Corpus Christi Fair, excursions to Helston for the famous floral dance on 8th May, or evening trips to Penzance or St. Ives, there were regular excursions including Sundays, to Plymouth at 5/- each from Penzance. Further afield, there were special excursion fares to London for the British Industries Fair, important football or rugby matches or, indeed, the Jubilee celebrations during May that year. The fare from Penzance was 21/6d and the service was, invariably, the 9.00 p.m. Jubilee celebrations also gave both Penzance and the GWR an ideal opportunity for positive publicity. A special consignment of flowers was sent to London in connection with the festivities to be displayed in a prominent shop window in Oxford Street, along with the following notice: 'These blooms were gathered from Morrab Gardens (Penzance) at 8 p.m. on Saturday 4th May, railed at 9 p.m. and displayed here at 8 a.m. on Sunday 5th May.'

In March, a special train ran from Penzance to Birkenhead in connection with the 'Grand National'. It departed at 7.30 p.m. and the fare was advertised at 22/6d. Finally, moving on to September 1938, a special excursion from Penzance to Glasgow is well worth consideration. It was organised in connection with the Glasgow Exhibition and departed Penzance at 3.05 p.m. on Friday 9th September. Arrival time at Buchanan Street, Glasgow, was 7.39 a.m. on the Saturday morning, and the 566 passengers enjoyed 14 hours in the city before returning home. Arrival time at Penzance was 3.00 p.m. on Sunday afternoon, marking the completion of a 1,182 mile journey overall, at an estimated cost of one penny for every three miles travelled!

GWR achievement overall was also the result of considerable research and development in locomotive design. G.J. Churchward and C.B. Collet were responsible for building a superb fleet of locomotives, capable of meeting the exacting demands of a distinguished railway company. Churchward's famous City 4-4-0s of 1903 and William Dean's Bulldog 4-4-0s, introduced in 1899, were regular motive power for the early *Cornish Riviera Express*. Churchward's 4-6-0 designs: the Stars 1906, and Saints from 1902, were the forerunners of Collett's

later Castles of 1923, and Halls of 1928. These locomotives were identified closely with services to and from the West of England, and the Kings as developed from 1927, were closely identified with *The Cornish Riviera*, between Paddington and Plymouth. The Granges of 1936, and the Manors of 1938 also had close associations with West Cornwall. In a positive hiearchy of the copper-capped chimney and Brunswick green livery, the Castles, Halls and Granges, in particular, were the mainstay of the regular traffic in the district, and the immediate choice for working the express goods trains, the mail and the milk. The Castles held pride of place on express workings, but in overall terms, the Cornish main line, with its fierce gradients, curvature, and general traffic requirements, made the Halls, and later the Granges, ideal motive power. On the branch-lines, also, Churchward's 4400 and 4500 class tanks of 1904 and 1906 became part of the order of things: the latter, at St. Ives, staying to the very end of steam working in the area.

To the layman, GWR locomotives were distinguished not only in appearance, but in name also. Their names displayed on imposing brass plates, were carefully chosen to suggest dignity, tradition and elegance. Their qualities of workmanship and performance were also a source of great pride to the company, and to the people they served, locally. It was yet another instance, often repeated, of the ways in which the GWR established itself as an institution in the West Country.

By the time the shadow of another World War had been cast across Europe, the GWR had established the pattern and practice for tourist traffic to the West Country. There had been heavy investment in anticipation of impressive returns, for perishables, as well as passengers; but, in the event, the war cut across all such expectations, precipitating fundamental long-term changes.

Protecting the railway and shoreline during the Second World War. Ponsandane signalbox with its distinctive flat roof is clearly visible here whilst work goes on in the defence of Mounts Bay. This photograph from very early in the War shows one of many defensive measures along the beach including machine gun emplacements and various other anti-personnel and anti tank devices.

Penzance Library

PENZANCE SUMMER WORKING — 1932

Paddington — Penzance Arrivals (Weekdays)

12.30 a.m.	Sats. only Holiday Ticket Train (dep. Padd. 4.38 p.m.).
7.40 a.m.	Sleeping Car Service 1st & 3rd Class (dep. Padd. 9.50 p.m.).
8.10 a.m.	FRI only Holiday Ticket Train (dep. Padd. 11.00 p.m.).
8.48 a.m.	Exeter, Plymouth—Penzance Express (dep. Padd. 1.40 a.m.).
10.55 a.m.	Sleeping Car Service (to Plymouth) (dep. Padd. 12 midnight).
3.40 p.m.	Via Bristol (dep. Padd. 5.30 a.m.).
4.05 p.m.	Fri/Sats ONLY Holiday Ticket Train (dep. Padd. 8.25 a.m.).
4.50 p.m.	'Cornish Riviera Express': branch (dep. Padd. 10.30 a.m.) connections, Falmouth arr. 4.38, Helston arr. 5.09 (The Lizard road motor arr. 6.10). St. Ives arr. 5.10 (Lands End road motor arr. 5.45).
6.30 p.m.	SAT only Luncheon and Tea Car Express (dep. Padd. 11.05 a.m.).
6.40 p.m.	SAT EXCEPTED Luncheon and Tea Car Express (dep. Padd. 11.05 a.m.).
9.30 p.m.	Luncheon, Tea, Dining Car Express (dep. Padd. 1.30 p.m.).

Penzance — Paddington Departures (Weekdays)

10.00 a.m.	'Cornish Riviera Express' (arr. Padd. 4.45 p.m.)
11.10 a.m.	Luncheon Tea & Dining Car Express (arr. Padd. 6.55 p.m.)
1.30 p.m.	Luncheon Tea & Dining Car Express (arr. Padd. 9.00 p.m.)
1.40 p.m.	SATS ONLY Holiday Ticket Train (arr. Padd. 10.00 p.m.)
8.10 p.m.	FRI ONLY Holiday Ticket Train (arr. Padd. 5.10 p.m.)
9.00 p.m.	Sleeping Car Service 1st and 3rd class (arr. Padd. 7.10 a.m.)

Paddington — Penzance: Return Fare, First Class 126/6; Third Class 76/–.
Single Fare, First Class 63/3; Third Class 38/–.

Midlands/North to Penzance Arrivals (Weekdays) — Penzance

10.00 a.m.	FRI ONLY Holiday Ticket Train Manchester Victoria dep. 8.55 p.m.
1.17 p.m.	'North Express' conveying through coaches from Manchester London Road, dep. 11.40 p.m., Liverpool dep. 10.45 p.m., Glasgow Cen 5.30.
5.55 p.m.	SATS ONLY Wolverhampton Express dep. 9.03 a.m.
6.40 p.m.	FRI ONLY Wolverhampton Express dep. 9.03 a.m.
7.30 p.m.	SATS EXCEPTED Wolverhampton and Birmingham Express Luncheon Tea and Dining Car Train dep. 10.40 a.m.)
7.40 p.m.	SATS ONLY Wolverhampton/Birmingham Express dep. 10.40 a.m.)

Penzance — Midlands/North Departures (Weekdays)

7.45 a.m.	SATS ONLY Birmingham Express arr. 4.25 p.m.
7.45 a.m.	SATS EXCEPTED Wolverhampton Express arrive 5.10 p.m. (Luncheon, Tea Car Workings)
10.15 a.m.	Birkenhead and Liverpool Lime Street (Luncheon Tea and Dining Service with through coach for Glasgow Central).
10.45 a.m.	Birmingham and Wolverhampton Express arr. 7.30 p.m. Luncheon Tea and Dining Service with through coaches for Edinburgh and Aberdeen.
12.30 p.m.	'North Express' — through coaches for Manchester London Road arr. 1.35 a.m., Liverpool Lime Street 1.05 a.m., Glasgow Central 6.45 a.m.
5.05 p.m.	Through services — Newport 12.28 a.m., Manchester London Road 6.05 a.m., Liverpool Lime Street 5.55 a.m.
5.55 p.m.	FRI ONLY Holiday Ticket Train Manchester London Road arr. 6.37 a.m.

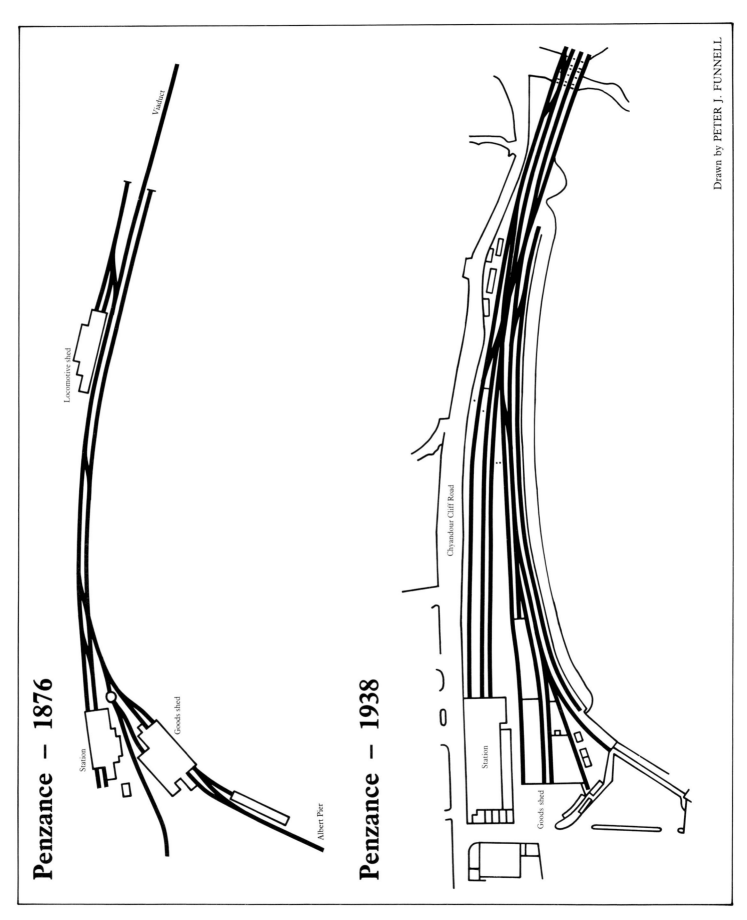

Penzance – 1876

Viaduct

Locomotive shed

Station

Goods shed

Albert Pier

Penzance – 1938

Chyandour Cliff Road

Station

Goods shed

Drawn by PETER J. FUNNELL

Chapter Four

Penzance: The Terminus

In April 1875 the local press described Penzance station as, 'a large dog's house of the nastiest and draughtiest kind'. This was one of many complaints about the poor conditions at the terminus, and with the opening of the new station at St. Ives in June 1877, criticism of Penzance was intensified. As the terminus of the broad gauge route from Paddington, the station had little to recommend it. It was totally inadequate to deal with the demands of any increased traffic, and it failed to reflect the image of a prosperous railway company, and an important market town.

Changes followed once the GWR took overall control in February 1876. In May that year extended goods accommodation was provided at a cost of £2,700 and a locomotive shed was also built to the east of the station at Chyandour. Within two years plans were completed for a new terminal building, and on 16th April 1878 the cutting of the first sod set detailed work underway.

The new station was much larger than the original and extended westward covering the site of a goods and coal yard. It required the construction of a new road immediately beyond the main building linking the harbour and the main street through the town. The town council agreed to widen Market Jew Street in the vicinity of the station to an overall width of 44 feet, with a thirty foot carriageway and two pathways of seven feet each. The GWR took responsibility for the main sewers serving the station

area. These were laid in 1878 whilst building was still in progress.

By November 1879 the new station had opened to traffic, but work was not completed until November, the following year. The contractors were Messrs Vernon and Ewens who had recently been employed at Torquay. All plans were drawn by the Design Office at Paddington, with costs estimated at £16,000.

The main building walls, fascias, sills and chimney stacks were of dressed granite, and an overall roof, 250 feet long with a span of 80 feet, provided covered accommodation for two platforms with a third line, between them for rolling stock. The roof was originally of corrugated iron, wooden boarding and glass, with a lantern light running the entire length. A moulded wooden windscreen was also set into the gable end, to form an elliptical arch decorating the rail approach to the building. The booking hall and offices faced Market Jew Street with an entrance at road level above the platforms. A large awning was also fixed over the entrance to the booking hall, the latter measuring twenty five feet by twenty feet with a large lantern in an open roof of varnished pitch-pine. The Stationmasters office was situated beyond the booking hall overlooking the main concourse. Stairs led down to the platforms where, beneath the booking hall, was a complete set of waiting rooms fitted with lavatories, and other conveniences. A refreshment room faced the arrival platform on the south side of the station close to the exit. The parcels office,

Penzance Station showing the original West Cornwall railway terminal building. The goods yard, enlarged in the mid 1870s, and the provision of mixed gauge. This fine view of the terminus, taken by an expert local photographer, shows the extremely restricted accommodation of the early years. Note also the interesting detail of the disc and crossbar signal at the end of the platform and the broad gauge locomotive opposite. Disc and crossbar signalling was a feature of the associated companies, whose influence in West Cornwall was important from 1865 onward. Prior to this the West Cornwall Company used semaphore signalling.
Penzance Town Council, Penlee House Museum

guard's room and porters' room were also situated on this side of the station. The lamp room was set into the opposite (northern) wall beneath Market Jew Street, where a hot water supply was also available.

With the end of the broad gauge the platforms were widened and lengthened and increased space made it possible to add a fourth line beneath the overall roof. In 1906 the Company again attempted to enlarge the station, but the plans were opposed by the council. During July of the following year the Great Western management warned of the problems that would follow if development at the station was delayed for any length of time. Traffic had reached an acute stage of congestion, sufficient for the General Manager to warn that 'great changes must be effected if the town is to maintain its commercial connections'. The Great Western had hoped to extend their site southward by enclosing a section of the shoreline, reclaiming it from the sea. This would provide valuable land to extend freight handling, which had always been a major part of the business at Penzance. Sidings were of course available on the quayside at Albert Pier, but overall, there was inadequate provision for the extent of trade.

The volume of traffic using the old goods yard at the station increased in the inter war years. Apart from specific movement of broccoli, potatoes, flowers and fish, there was livestock, animal feed, fruit traffic and the general merchandise of the town. The large retail traders such as Allied Suppliers had regular deliveries on Monday mornings. Fruit traffic for the principal retailers in the town and consignments for outfitters, chemists and the footwear trade for example, all relied upon the railway and its over-worked goods department at the station.

Regular deliveries were made around the town, which was divided into five main districts for the purpose. Beyond this, areas such as St. Buryan, Land's End, St. Just and Pendeen, received deliveries twice or three times a week. The Newlyn and Mousehole district, like Penzance, enjoyed daily services. Stables for the horses used on deliveries were in Mount Street, as was the garage for the Company buses. Mount Street is immediately opposite the former main entrance to the station.

There was a regular trade in livestock. Penzance had always been an important market town with regular markets held on Thursdays and Saturdays. (Nowadays on Tuesdays and Thursdays.) Large numbers of cattle and pigs were sold and moved on these days. There was regular trade between the local markets, such as Truro, from where cattle were sent each Wednesday for slaughter at Penzance. Special refrigerated vans MICA 'A' or 'B' also conveyed slaughtered calves to Plymouth on Thursdays after the market. These were worked on the 7.20 p.m. partially fitted goods to Plymouth. Animal feed from Avonmouth was also an important traffic.

The goods accommodation dated largely from the 1870s, with certain alterations during the rebuilding of the station in 1879/1880. There were three covered roads, one leading through the shed to Albert Pier. The latter was nearest the sea wall and next to it was the inward goods line. These two were separated by a narrow platform where beer traffic, in particular, was unloaded. The third line serving the outward goods platform was separated by a roadway, and, of course, the platform itself. Sliding doors in the far wall gave access to one of the lines serving the loading bay in the yard outside.

The yard separated the passenger and goods accommodation. It consisted of a vee shaped loading platform served by two lines: that nearest the shed, number one, being known locally as the 'short siding'; the other number two, as the 'fish siding'. The latter originally connected with a large granary behind the station and was officially called 'Hosking's Siding'. The majority of the flower and fish traffic was loaded from these platforms. A crane was installed on the platform and a weighbridge and office was situated at the entrance to the yard near the exit from the passenger station. The main goods offices were in the shed itself, but an examiner's hut was located at the head of the 'fish siding' and a shunter's cabin at the entrance to the goods depot, opposite number two passenger platform. The goods lines ran immediately to the south of this passenger platform and they were separated by a wooden fence. The entire complex disappeared in the rebuilding programme, which obviously included the provision of the new purpose built goods shed at Ponsandane.

A new layout was planned for the terminus with extended platform space and additional land for sidings to the south. By the 1930s it had become necessary to start certain trains from St. Erth because of the lack of space at Penzance. This was obviously unsatisfactory for the image of a company like the GWR. As the terminus for the celebrated West of England line and, therefore, the destination of the prestigious Cornish Riviera Express, it was essential that Penzance station should reflect the appropriate atmosphere. Work began early in 1937.

By summer the new layout was taking shape. Four platform faces were provided, each one able to cope with a twelve-coach train comfortably. Numbers three and four were shorter than the other two, because of the access required to the loading bays in the yard. To provide the land for the new yard vast amounts of rock and filling was used claiming ground from the sea. The original sea wall was breached to the west of the Chyandour river, opposite the present signal box. A breakwater was constructed and infilling then took place in a south-westerly direction towards Albert Pier. The break or overlap in the sea wall marks the site where the new work began. It was obviously difficult work during the winter, but on the night of Monday 30th July 1937 work began on the construction of the sea wall. Eighty men were employed on this and as a part of the project they were to build a twelve feet wide promenade to run for over 1,000 feet from Albert Pier to Chyandour. The latter was included under the GWR Additional Powers Act 1937. It was the intention to give extended pedestrian access to the waterside, making it possible to walk from Newlyn to Marazion along the seashore. This would certainly have given improved access to the Eastern Green beach, which despite its proximity to the town, was never developed. The promenade was to be separated from the sidings by railings, and was certain to enhance the character of the station as a holiday terminal. Unfortunately it was never built, but the sea wall was completed, and did allow for excellent views across Mounts Bay towards the Lizard Peninsula.

The new terminus was given extra protection from storm damage by a shelving bank of boulders against the sea wall, as had been done for the embankment in 1921. The stone came from Princetown and Penryn, and was stored on bogie wagons at Marazion to be used as required. In recent years it has been further strengthened.

Reclamation of land below the shoreline made it possible to provide four station sidings (and four bays when vans used platform 4) with two sidings also reaching eastwards along the south or sea side of the embankment. These were inevitably known as the 'sea sidings' and direct access was available from each platform in the station. A crossover was also installed for locomotives using platforms 2 and 3 in order that they could run round their trains to return to the shed. As a result of this the majority of 'down' trains used these two platforms whilst numbers one and four dealt with a larger number of departures. Perishable traffic used platforms three and four because of the access for lorries and vans. The Mail always leaves from platform four because of this.

Two views showing the rebuilding and enlargement of Penzance station undertaken from 1937. The new sea wall is here under construction guarding the new ground, south of the old site, from the sea. By claiming land from the seaward side the station area overall was much enlarged giving spacious new facilities for perishable traffic operating from its own platform. The new passenger platform layout giving four lengthy faces can be seen getting underway towards the top left of the photographs and whilst the sea wall and embankment of 1921 can also be seen in the upper background. A promenade running along the top of the sea wall was intended to link the town area with the Eastern Green beach but this project unfortunately never materialised.   *Penzance Library*

Activity at the terminus. P. Gray's fine view of Penzance in July 1962, shows steam power almost at the very end; Long Rock depot closed to steam two months later. 'County' class No. 1001 *County of Bucks* waits at the head of the 4.45 p.m. to Manchester on Platform Two. DMU services (platform 4) had made significant inroads locally by this time and a diesel shunter had replaced steam in the yard. No other location in Britain gave a better view of train working than at Penzance. The photograph also reveals the extent of reconstruction work carried out by the GWR in 1937. The steam crane was often used on the raised section of track far left to repair and maintain the wall. Note the boulders beyond, as defence against the sea. Milk, flowers, fish and other perishable traffic was handled in the goods section under covered accommodation well illustrated in this photograph beyond the DMU.

P. Gray

Number four platform was particularly useful in that vans nearest the buffers could be loaded from both sides by also using number one bay. All the bay platforms and a section of platform four had their rails set in a concrete base fitted with drainage. This was for loading and servicing fish vans and similar traffic. The bay platforms were also covered for protection from the weather, giving a high standard of accommodation overall. The original goods yard and loading bay later became the main terminal for Western National buses to the great benefit of all those people requiring the use of bus and train.

With a complete change in the layout resignalling was essential. A new signal box opened on the site of the old locomotive depot in April 1938, controlling all movements in the station area as far as Ponsandane.

Penzance gained a spacious modern terminus as a result of GWR investment. At the annual Chamber of Commerce banquet in January 1938 the Company Superintendant gave the costs for the work overall as £134,000. For the decade or so following World War Two, traffic to and from Penzance more than justified this investment in the town.

On summer Saturdays in particular Penzance station often found it difficult to cope with the volume of tourist traffic and

siding accommodation for empty stock was at a premium. The goods bays at Ponsandane were in constant use, along with all available space in the vicinity of the goods shed. Empty stock trains made frequent trips to Marazion yard and to the sidings along the marsh. St. Erth yard and the refuge sidings at either end of the station were also taken. By the evening, at the height of the season, empty stock trains were often sent as far as Gwinear Road in order to give working room at the terminus.

For normal weekday service, Penzance station, Ponsandane and Marazion each had their own shunters. Shunting was always in progress during the day, making or dividing a whole range of trains, but this is not required to any great extent today as most trains work in specific sets. A shunter does work though between the station and Ponsandane yard, mainly for the transfer of stock to and from the sidings.

The last decade has brought considerable change at the terminus. A purpose built HST depot has replaced the old locomotive shed at Long Rock, and new sidings have been installed there. Prior to this, the main line was singled, west of Marazion and all semaphore signalling disappeared with the resignalling project and the alterations to the layout generally. Two sidings in the station yard have only recently been lifted. One nearest the

Above: Penzance station looking eastward from the raised booking hall balcony. The walls and overall roof date from the rebuilding programme of 1879/1880. The platforms and track plan dates from 1937. Note the extreme length of the platform built for heavy tourist traffic.

Right: A further view from the balcony showing something of the main circulating area beyond the buffer stop and Wyman's bookstall. The parcels office can also be seen opposite the bookstall.

The 'Royal Mail' set on platform four in the late afternoon. This train always used platform four because of easy access for Post Office vehicles. The locomotive for this train at the time (the very early 1960s) was that which had worked in on the 'down' Cornish Riviera Express arriving at 4.55 p.m. The 'Mail' departed at 7.00 p.m.

All photos Lens of Sutton

Penzance at Midday. No. 4955 *Plaspower Hall* backs out of No. 3 platform with the empty stock from the 11.50 a.m. arrival from Newton Abbot on 11th May 1959. On the left, in platform No. 2, is the stock for the 1.20 p.m. departure for Paddington. *M. Mensing*

Plaspower Hall almost at the buffers on Platform One on 11th May 1959. The train was the 11.50 arrival from Newton Abbot. Beyond the loco are the two suburban coaches forming the 3.35 stopping service to Truro. *M. Mensing*

'Castle' class No. 4095 *Harlech Castle* at platform No. 1 with the 11.00 a.m. departure, *The Royal Duchy*, for Paddington on Easter Monday 1958. Note the incomplete headcode, with the missing lamp. With the onset of diesel working, double-headed Class 22 locomotives in the D63XX series regularly worked this service, returning westward from Plymouth on the 'down' *Royal Duchy* arriving in Penzance at 9.20 p.m.

P.Q. Treloar

sea wall, originally gave access to the Albert Pier, and the other was the end bay, last used to stable locomotives. Freight traffic has also ceased and Ponsandane goods depot is closed, but passenger and perishable traffic still does well. The summer timetable in particular is most encouraging, offering a wide ranging service linked to the image of the High Speed Train.

Penzance station has recently been modernised. On 28th November 1980, The Queen unveiled a plaque to mark the centenary of the main building. All the stonework was examined and cleaned, and detailed improvements were carried out on the main concourse. A new travel centre was opened on 4th November 1983 on the site of the former telegraph office and refreshment rooms. The old booking hall and offices overlooking the platform

were then closed, bringing everything on to one level. The former main entrance to the station and the stairway are therefore no longer in use. A new refreshment room, waiting room and bookstall have also been built immediately in front of the original waiting rooms, and on platforms three and four new offices were opened in December 1982 for the Traffic Assistant and the Movements staff.

The prevailing atmosphere at Penzance station is that of a busy working terminus; the railhead for the Land's End peninsula. Its particular appeal is probably the combination of its excellent position on the shores of Mounts Bay and the fact that it is the terminus; the most westerly point on the railway in mainland Britain.

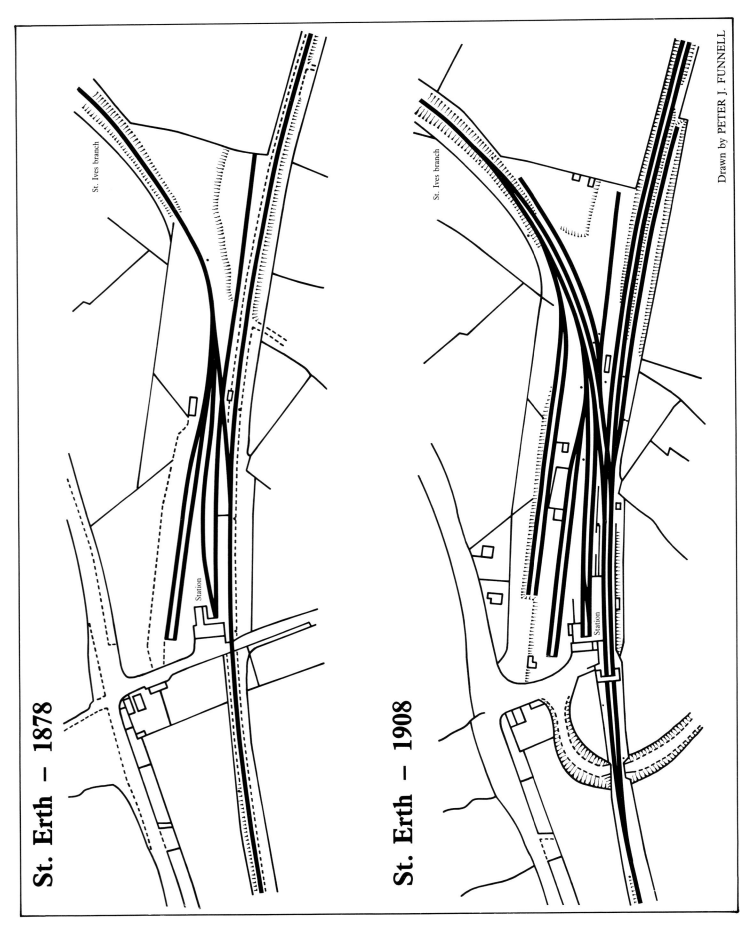

St. Erth – 1878

St. Erth – 1908

St. Ives branch

Station

Drawn by PETER J. FUNNELL

Chapter Five

The St. Ives Branch

The 4¼ mile branch line from St. Erth to St. Ives opened to traffic on 1st June 1877. To mark the occasion, a special train consisting of six coaches and a saloon, headed by a locomotive, *Elephant*, left Penzance at 11 a.m., forming the inaugural service. The train, carrying important civic and railway officials, was suitably decorated with flags and garlands and was met at St Ives in celebration by the Band of the 11th and 13th Duke of Cornwall Volunteers. History was made; not only in the opening of a railway to the town, but also in that this particular branch was the last broad gauge line to be built.

The branch was authorised as part of the West Cornwall Railway under the Act of Parliament of 7th July 1873. Work then proceeded with the appointment of the contractor, Thomas Lang, of Plymouth, who also built Lelant Quay. There had been possibilities for an earlier line to St. Ives in the details of the

together with two viaducts, at Carbis Bay and St. Ives; there were also great contrasts between the easier workings across the sand dunes near Lelant, for instance, and the headlands, where deep cuttings were driven through the greenstone.

On completion the line was extremely spectacular and it soon began to attract the attention of the tourists. It also provided a valuable service to the fishing industry at St. Ives. From 1st August 1878 it became the property of the GWR and under its management the branch progressed to become one of the most important holiday lines in Britain. The purchase of the Tregenna Castle Hotel by the GWR showed that the Company meant to develop the town as an important resort from the beginning.

St. Erth became an imposing and spacious junction. An entirely new station was built in dressed granite, which included platforms for 'up' and 'down' main line services and a bay for the

St Erth looking toward Penzance in the 1920s. This station, originally known at St Ives Road, was rebuilt in 1876 and still retains much of its GWR character even today. The flower-bed and palm trees added to the 'Riviera' atmosphere, actively encouraged by Great Western management. The St Ives bay platform and the goods yard were to the right of the camera. *Cornwall County Museum*

original Act of 1846, whereby the Hayle Railway was purchased by the West Cornwall Company. Plans involved crossing the estuary from the Hayle direction, but in the event, the Admiralty expressed its total opposition and the idea was dropped.

Construction over the 4¼ mile route entailed heavy engineering work, but building was well in hand by the summer of 1875. The junction at St. Erth previously known as St. Ives Road, required a substantial yard, and a new station complex generally. Numerous cuttings and embankments were necessary

branch trains on the 'up' or north side of the line. Separate waiting accommodation was provided for ladies in first or third class, together with a general waiting room, stationmaster's office, parcels office and booking hall. To satisfy requirements for the yard, the rising ground to the north of the original station was levelled for goods platforms and sidings. Additional sidings were also provided at the east end of the station on the 'down' side, parallel to the main line. A signal box was opened at the east end of the station. It was fitted with 32 levers controlling the main

'4500' class 2-6-2 No. 4540 runs round its stock in the bay platform at St Erth on 24th July 1957. As it is the busy summer period the normal two-coach suburban set has been strengthened with corridor stock. St Erth creamery can be seen on the left. This supplied a great deal of milk traffic to Kensington.
P. Gray

Nos. 4549 and 4570 have double-headed the stock of the *Cornish Riviera Express* off the branch in the late afternoon, 30th July 1960. They are seen here returning to the branch as indicated by the shunting signal displaying 'up branch'. The Riviera stock has been stored in the 'down' refuge sidings opposite the signalbox. At the west end of the station there was also an 'up' refuge, sufficient to cope with the ten coaches of the 'Limited'. Dining.cars were often stored there on Fridays for the rush of workings eastward the next day. No. 4549 has its number on the buffer beam and displays the earlier BR 'Lion and Wheel' emblem. Note the Penzance shed code -83G- prominent on the smokebox door.
P. Gray

Left: The bay platform area for St Ives trains at St Erth. A '4500' class locomotive shunts on the goods line. The booking office, parcels office and waiting rooms are in the main building behind the people and the brake van.
Lens of Sutton

Below: Engine crew, guard, station staff and passengers are all posing for the camera at Lelant in the early years of this century. The train is for Carbis Bay and St Ives; note the observation blisters on the coaching stock.
Cornwall County Museum

line, branch and yard movements, and was worked on shifts from 6 a.m. to 3 p.m. and 3 p.m. to Midnight.

Leaving St. Erth the branch curves away northward in the 'up' direction from the main line and descends through a cutting on a 1 in 62 gradient to meet the upper reaches of the Hayle estuary. From this point the line keeps very close contact with water; either alongside the estuary, or on the cliffs above the open sea. An embankment carried the line over the upper reaches of the estuary to Lelant at its northern end. The embankment was made with the spoil from the cutting preceeding it. (A tramway was used to carry the soil.)

Lelant was the only wooden station on the line and was built on a foundation of concrete 8 feet deep. First and second class waiting rooms together with a third class general waiting room and a booking hall were provided on the single platform. A small signal box was also built in connection with the traffic to the quay nearby, and was fitted with eleven levers. The line to the quay curved away from the north end of the station on an embankment, following the shoreline. Lelant Quay was a granite construction over 600 feet long and included warehouses, a steam crane and a weighbridge. In October 1888 a standard gauge line

The wooden structure of Lelant station building. This view compares well with that on page 10 taken in broad gauge days. The only notable alterations are the addition of new iron railings and a new style station sign.   *Lens of Sutton*

Here was the first contact with the Atlantic shore, the rolling breakers and sea wind, and from this point, the line continues its climb at 1 in 60 on an embankment across the dunes. This embankment used the spoil, largely sand, from the cutting preceeding it, and in the case of structures such as these, the banks were turfed to give greater stability.

At the far end of the embankment the line reaches a summit and enters Carrack Gladden cutting. It was a formidable task cutting through this headland separating Lelant and Carbis Bay beaches, indeed, it was considered the most difficult work on the entire line. After blasting and clearing through greenstone in a cutting some 57 feet deep the line curves inland, to reach Carbis Bay (three miles).

Carbis Bay station was a split level development with single platform. The booking office was situated on the approach road above the station and the waiting room was below on the platform itself. The reason for this was the restricted site available, the station being in a cutting. Immediately beyond the platform the line crosses the steep Carbis Valley giving its name to the imposing three piered viaduct carrying the line. Like all the granite used in constructing the line this stone came from quarries locally, at Towednack, near St. Ives. The four arches of this structure each had a span of 40 feet and reached 78 feet in height.

Between Carbis Bay and St. Ives the line again climbs to a further cutting at Porthminster Headland, this being some 30 feet deep. This section of the line also crossed old mine workings with some levels driven out under the sea. From the cutting the line descends to cross Porthminster viaduct and enters the terminus itself.

was extended from St. Erth to the quay, providing mixed gauge working until 1892.

Beyond Lelant the rising gradient of 1 in 60 lifts the line through a sand based cutting out onto the famous sand dunes – a fascinating open expanse that allows spectacular views seaward. *The Homeland Handbook* declared: 'Beyond the cutting there breaks upon the sight a view so beautiful and of a quality of happiness so unusual as to commend itself warmly to the traveller'.

Nos. 4566 and 4563 leaving Lelant with the stock for the 9.20 a.m. St Ives — Paddington. With both 'up' and 'down' services on summer saturdays the coaching stock was worked as a service on the branch, but ran ECS between St Erth and Penzance. The old alignment to Lelant Quay — mixed gauge from St Erth from 1888 — can be seen on the shoreline in the foreground. 9th September 1961.   *P. Gray*

The *Cornish Riviera Express* crossing Lelant dunes double-headed by '4500' class locomotives Nos. 4554 and 4568 on 30th August 1958. Ten coaches was the maximum load allowed on the branch. The gradient here is 1 in 60 and is clearly making the locomotives work hard. Hayle power station is in the background.   *P. Gray*

Local branch train waiting at Carbis Bay en route to the junction, 30th July 1960. Carbis Bay was a split-site station with the waiting room on the platform and the booking office above on more open ground. Hotels, cliffs and beach emphasise the lines identity with tourism. Notice also the station name set in painted stones in the cutting facing the platform.   *P. Gray*

The station buildings at St. Ives were 120 feet long and 25 feet wide, and were built of dressed granite. They compared very favourably with the terminal arrangements at Penzance at that particular time. The booking hall was reached through an entrance to the rear of the building and independant first and third class waiting rooms for ladies were provided. Together with a general waiting room, a refreshment room, 25 feet by 19 feet was included, with a kitchen and beer cellar, described as 'a saloon compared to the 'hut' at Penzance'. A parcels office and stationmaster's accommodation was also situated in this main building.

A locomotive shed was built beyond the viaduct and to the west of the line approaching St. Ives. The site, prepared by cutting and clearing against the cliffside, included a small workshop, offices and a water-tower. This was a small sub-shed to Penzance and was useful for overnight stabling, and light maintenance. A signal box was set back against the western boundary of the station site close by the rail access to the goods yard, approximately mid-way between the station buildings and the viaduct.

The goods shed was set back towards the cliff wall, alongside the station. Two goods lines served a wide platform

Above: Carbis Bay looking towards St Ives. This view from the post-war period shows the split-site arrangement required, as the station was built in a cutting. The ticket office is in the area above the cutting and the waiting room is on the platform. Modern housing gradually encroaches on the open fields beyond.
Lens of Sutton

Right: A busy scene at St Ives in the 1950s. Both trains are formed of corridor stock, the incoming service being made up of seven coaches. The normal 'B' set stock is in the siding near the buffer stops.
Lens of Sutton

St. Ives – 1908

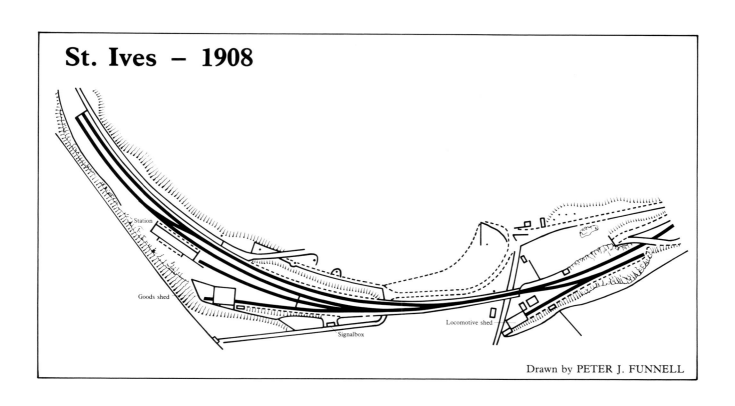

Station

Goods shed

Signalbox

Locomotive shed

Drawn by PETER J. FUNNELL

No. 4566 waits to depart from St. Ives on 13th September 1959 for St. Erth. Note the massive granite cliff wall behind the station and the occupied camping coach on the left-hand side. *J.E. Bell*

area, with one of the lines connecting into the shed. A short bay platform was often used for wagons and for storing coaches, but it was also clearly marked out for passenger traffic. On the passenger platforms an extra four feet in width was gained when the broad gauge was abolished, but the station was very well provided with one extended platform face eventually over 500 feet long. This was fitted with a crossover and loop to allow for locomotives to run round their train, or for two trains to take occupation of the platform face simultaneously.

A broad approach road curved down to the platform area from the main road on the hillside above the station, and heavy retaining walls were built to the front and rear. A flight of steps was cut into the cliff wall at the rear of the station for pedestrian access to and from the road into the town. A weighbridge was also installed beside the wide station gate at the entrance to the site.

The train service as operated from the first week of June 1877 was as follows:

Weekdays

St Erth	10.30	2.40	4.10	7.00	9.50
Lelant	10.33	2.44	4.13	7.03	9.53
Carbis Bay	10.41	2.52	4.21	7.11	—
St Ives	10.45	2.56	4.25	7.15	10.03
St Ives	9.55	1.00	3.40	6.25	9.25
Carbis Bay	9.58	1.04	3.44	6.28	9.28
Lelant	10.06	1.12	3.52	6.36	9.36
St Erth	10.10	1.16	3.55	6.40	9.40

Sundays p.m. Only

St Ives	3.40	5.50	St Erth	4.10	6.20
Carbis Bay	3.44	5.54	Lelant	4.13	6.23
Lelant	3.52	6.02	Carbis Bay	4.21	6.31
St Erth	3.55	6.05	St Ives	4.25	6.35

By 1909 the service was again extended.

Journey time was fifteen minutes and a maximum speed limit of 30 m.p.h. was set for the line. On freight workings trains were required to stop at both Porthminster Point and Carrack Gladden, above Carbis Bay, in order to pin down brakes, in view of the descent from these particular locations. Freight traffic off the branch could be extremely heavy, particularly fish; in December 1898, for example, 500 tons of herrings were moved from St. Ives alone in one day.

Less than one month after opening to traffic, the line was attracting tourists. On 28th June *The West Briton* reported that lodgings were, 'exceedingly scarce at Carbis Bay and St. Ives owing to the influx of strangers'. In the following month there was a further report: 'Many visitors have been compelled to leave St. Ives because of the lack of accommodation'. By 1898, however, the newspaper reported very satisfactory arrangements:

'We are glad to learn that large numbers of visitors are now arriving at St. Ives. All those who visited us last year are returning to the hotels where they were so well catered for. Perhaps there is no small line of railway in the kingdom where there are so many trains running in and out as at St. Ives; there being no less than nineteen trains every day, commencing at 7.20 a.m. and leaving off at 9.17 at night. The trains keep remarkably good time and are well filled.'

Tourism was frequently in conflict with the fishing industry, often over the problem of the smell from the fish. The famous Parson Kilvert, considered this smell sufficient, on occasion, to 'stop the church clock'! Fishing boats also occupied a great deal of the beach area, and their nets were set there to dry. The pattern of tourist traffic to St. Ives in the early years of the twentieth century was described by G.E. Mitton in his book *Cornwall* (1915).

'The season is only for two months of the year, August and September, during which months the place is packed and the numerous inhabitants who live on this yearly godsend of the 'foreigners' money are hard put to it to supply accommodation; but all year round there is a certain number of visitors who find in the clean fresh air, the glorious golf links, second to none, and, the wide views, just what they need.'

ST ERTH — ST IVES — OCTOBER 1909

WEEKDAYS					*		*		*						**Sundays**			
ST ERTH	7.25	8.20	9.10	10.00	11.00	12.50	2.33	3.40	5.05	5.52	6.55	8.47	9.32	7.25	8.40	3.00	5.45
LELANT	7.28	8.23	9.15	10.02	11.03	12.56	2.36	3.45	5.08	5.55	6.58	8.50	9.35	7.28	8.43	3.03	5.48
CARBIS BAY	7.36	8.31	9.25	10.10	11.11	1.05	2.44	3.53	5.15	6.02	7.06	8.58	9.42	7.36	8.51	3.11	5.56
ST IVES	7.40	8.35	9.30	10.14	11.15	1.12	2.48	3.58	5.20	6.07	7.10	9.02	9.47	7.40	8.55	3.15	6.00

					*	*	*								**Sundays**			
ST IVES	6.55	7.55	8.40	9.40	10.25	11.50	1.50	2.53	4.25	5.30	6.15	8.15	9.08	6.55	8.15	2.30	4.55
CARBIS BAY	7.00	8.00	8.45	9.45	10.30	11.55	1.55	2.58	4.30	5.35	6.20	8.20	9.13	7.00	8.20	2.35	5.00
LELANT	7.06	8.06	8.50	9.51	10.36	12.00	2.02	3.04	4.36	5.41	6.26	8.26	9.19	7.06	8.26	2.41	5.06
ST ERTH	7.10	8.10	8.55	9.55	10.40	12.07	2.08	3.08	4.40	5.45	6.30	8.30	9.23	7.10	8.30	2.45	5.10

* MIXED TRAINS.

An excellent view of St. Ives loco shed in the early morning of 9th September 1961. No. 4564 was the last engine to spend the night at the small sub shed to Penzance (83G). It is clearly the end of an era, but note how well the site is maintained; all in the best traditions of the GWR. Details such as the gas lamp, and the ladder and hose stored against the wall give added interest in a fine composition.   *P. Gray*

TIMETABLE: SATURDAYS SUMMER 1959

											*								
ST ERTH		6.35	7.48	8.40	9.36	10.20	11.17	12.05	1.30	2.15	2.45	3.55	4.40	5.15	6.25	6.50	7.35	8.15	9.00	9.45	10.40
LELANT		6.38	7.51	8.43	—	—	11.20	12.08	1.33	2.18	2.48	3.58	4.43	5.18	6.28	6.53	7.38	8.18	9.03	9.48	10.43
CARBIS BAY	6.13	6.45	7.58	8.50	9.44	10.28	11.27	12.15	1.40	2.25	2.55	4.05	4.50	5.25	6.35	7.00	7.45	8.25	9.10	9.55	10.50
ST IVES	6.20	6.53	8.03	8.57	9.50	10.34	11.32	12.20	1.45	2.30	3.00	4.10	4.55	5.35	6.40	7.05	7.50	8.30	9.15	10.00	10.55

* CORNISH RIVIERA EXPRESS

					*												
ST IVES	5.45	7.25	8.10	9.20	9.55	10.40	10.55	11.40	1.05	1.50	3.30	4.20	5.45	7.10	7.55	8.35	9.20
CARBIS BAY	5.50	7.30	8.15	9.25	10.00	10.45	11.00	11.45	1.10	1.55	3.35	4.25	5.50	7.15	8.00	8.40	9.25
LELANT	—	7.36	8.21	9.31	10.06	—	11.06	11.51	1.16	2.01	3.41	4.31	5.56	7.21	8.06	8.46	9.31
ST ERTH	6.00	7.40	8.25	9.35	10.10	10.53	11.10	11.55	1.20	2.05	3.45	4.35	6.00	7.25	8.10	8.50	9.35

The GWR was eager to promote business, and once they had taken control of the branch in 1878, they negotiated the most prestigious accommodation at St. Ives, namely the castelled mansion house of the Stephens family in its park setting of one hundred acres. This was to be the GWR showpiece: the Treganna Castle Hotel. Accommodation could be arranged by telegraph from any Great Western station and all trains were met by the hotel porter. During 1929 the company placed a contract for extensions to the premises at a cost of £35,000 thereby indicating the value of tourist traffic at St. Ives. An exclusive hotel estate with farm and gardens guaranteed their supply of vegetables and dairy produce, and helped to develop the sense of distinction and style that was characteristic of this hotel.

The GWR made a particular point of promoting the unique features of the branch itself. Indeed, the special character of the train journey from St. Erth was used to good effect. *The Homeland Handbook* claimed:

> 'The branch from St. Erth to St. Ives is such as to make the traveller rejoice at the glories it affords of the pleasant places amongst which his days are to be spent. But to get the best view in all its beauty, choose a corner seat on the right of the carriage facing the engine.'

In summer months, as increasingly heavier trains struggled with the gradient across Lelant dunes or beyond Carbis Bay for Porthminster Point, the GWR drew a certain satisfaction from knowing that one of its most powerful attractions was the view enjoyed immediately beyond the carriage window. More explicit promotion came through the pages of *The Cornish Riviera* (1904), *Holiday Haunts* (1906), *The Ocean Coast* (1925) and an entirely new version of *The Cornish Riviera* in August 1928 written by S.P. Mais.

By the third decade of this century St. Ives was served by through coaches on the *Cornish Riviera Express* and the summer timetable for 1932 showed seventeen trains to St. Ives and fifteen to St. Erth. The first train of the day was the 7.05 departure from St. Ives and the last, the 9.25 p.m. from St. Erth. On Sundays, services to and from St. Ives were worked by the Road Motor Car with five journeys in each direction. This run took 22 minutes in both directions, it being stated that 'heavy luggage is not conveyed'. Fares from Paddington to St. Ives at that time were: First Class return - 125s. 0d. (£6.29) and Third Class 75s. 6d. (£3.77½p). In 1935 St. Ives was given enhanced status by the GWR when *The Cornish Riviera* ran on its new schedule, making St. Erth its only official stop from Paddington to Penzance. Locally there were regular excursions on the branch from all parts of West Cornwall.

The introduction of the Holidays and Pay Act in 1938 was important to the GWR and traffic to the West of England. In the following year some 11 million people were entitled to one week paid holiday, but the outbreak of war prevented the new arrangements from developing, at least, until peace returned. By that time, however, it was too late, as far as the Great Western was concerned; but for fifteen years or so of post war working, the branch carried its heaviest ever traffic in holiday-makers to its beaches, reaching its peak in the later 1950s.

At this time *The Cornish Riviera* ran direct to and from St. Ives with its maximum of ten coaches double-headed along the branch. The St. Ives departure for Paddington was at 9.20 a.m. arriving at 4.40 p.m. whilst the 10.30 a.m. departure from Paddington was timed to arrive at St. Ives at 5.35 p.m. This stock was then worked back to Penzance for servicing. At the height of the season (1959) through coaches for St. Ives departed Paddington at 10.12 p.m. on Friday night, arriving St. Ives 6.20 a.m. (11th –18th August). An unusual service over the branch in this period was the weekday (summer) 6.00 p.m. Penzance to

Truro stopping service via St. Ives. This train was often worked by a Churchward Mogul which waited at St. Erth yard whilst the 4500 class tanks worked the train over the branch. Arrival time at Truro was 8.08 p.m.

Numerous Sunday School specials used the branch even from the earliest days. Carbis Bay was a popular venue for these workings as this resort had purpose built tea rooms and gardens to cater for such events. Another popular working, this time on Sundays, during summer, was the 3.00 p.m. through train from Penzance to St. Ives with its return working at 7.20 p.m. allowing for 3½ hours at the resort. In the summer timetable for 1959, the weekday service provided sixteen trains to St. Ives and fifteen to St. Erth. On Sundays there were thirteen departures from St. Erth and twelve trains from St. Ives. The Saturday service comprised twenty one trains from St. Erth and seventeen from St. Ives.

Regular train working on the branch usually consisted of two suburban coaches when traffic was light, but in summer, four or five coach trains were provided, according to demand. Coaching stock was stored at the terminus on the lines beyond the crossing loop, leading to the buffer stops. Motive power on the line during the last decade of steam included Nos. 4540, 4545, 4548, 4549, 4561, 4563, 4564, 4566, 4570 and 4571. (The heavier '4575' versions of the 2-6-2T did not work the line.) These locomotives, all officially shedded at Penzance (83G) also performed duties on the Helston branch. Steam power at St. Ives disappeared in 1961 and the small locomotive depot closed during September. In the following year Penzance shed officially closed to steam, marking the end of an era in West Cornwall.

The publication of the Beeching Plan in 1963 marked the decisive watershed, in West Cornwall, as elsewhere. St. Ives was listed for closure but was reprieved, given the implementation of strict economies in working practice, which then transformed the character and appearance of the branch. It is also worth noting that in competition with rail travel at this time, the number of cars on the road began their phenomenal rise from under four million in 1959 to some sixteen million by the beginning of the 1970s. This particular period was, therefore, far more significant in its long-term effects on the branch than that of nationalisation in 1948.

To outward appearances there was little in the way of detailed change following the demise of the GWR. The years following nationalisation saw not a decisive break with the past, but a continuation after the pattern set by GWR, culminating in the record levels for traffic in the later 1950s. Fifteen years on, the opposite was true, and the changes, when they came, were all the more apparent because of the contrasts between the two very different sets of circumstances.

The relegation of the branch followed rapidly. By 1964 freight traffic had ceased and the branch was by then effectively reduced to a single line overall. From October 1963 the run-round loop fell into neglect and sidings and yard facilities were disregarded until demolition in 1966. The signal box disappeared when points and signalling were no longer required. Fixed distants were, however, retained as the only signals on the branch. Finally in May 1971, the main station buildings at the terminus were demolished in order to make way for a new car park. Carbis Bay and Lelant had also been relegated to unstaffed halts, the latter becoming a private house.

The presence of the railway above Porthminster Beach has now been largely eclipsed by an extensive car park and the aesthetic quality of the railway setting on a curve of rising ground above the beach, has also been destroyed. By way of replacement for the old granite station, British Rail have provided a single concrete platform with a shelter and seats on the alignment of the former goods yard. Beyond the buffer stop there is also a small

A local service entering St Ives with No. 4570, 4th August 1961. There is great detail here: the loco shed and viaduct on the approach to the station, loading gauge, signalbox, camping coach and goods shed. Note also the GWR 'Full Harp' design gas lights on the platform. Did the guests at the Trevessa Hotel, opposite, appreciate all this? Only the line on the far right beside the signalbox now remains: it is the site of the present day terminus. A car park now has priority! *P. Gray*

booking office, but the arrangements overall make for an impoverished substitute when compared with the past.

As from May 1978 a Park and Ride scheme has been in operation during the season, from a specially prepared site at Lelant Saltings, at the head of the estuary. This is well situated to take traffic from new road developments in the district and ample parking is available. The station is a single platform that overlooks the estuary just over a quarter of a mile south of the old Lelant station. The new service offered a combined parking and train ticket for up to nine people with a lively schedule of trains to the terminus on Saturdays. Signalling has also returned to the branch with this development.

In contrast, Lelant station itself now has a much reduced service and is slipping gradually into obscurity. Even so, it still reflects something of the overall spirit of the line, best represented in its Victorian and Edwardian residences with their conifers, fishponds, and quiet lawns.

At Carbis Bay where, in the 1950s, the station name was picked out in painted stone on the cutting opposite the platform, there is now no more than an isolated shelter on the platform. Other buildings have long since been demolished, leaving this

once charming and confident seaside location decidedly empty and forlorn.

St. Erth, however, is still in remarkably good shape. The original station buildings are intact and well cared for. Palm trees and a profusion of plants make this a very colourful location. Although the yard has now been lifted, the atmosphere of the junction is still very real. The bay platform, a magnificent footbridge, signal box, and semaphore signals all help to convey the image of a classic GWR country junction. The booking office, in particular, retains its earlier character as does the parcels office, where, in both cases, the best traditions of the past have been carefully preserved in a normal working environment. Collectively, therefore, these distinctive features at St. Erth represent the closest approximation today to the spirit of the GWR and its promotion of the Cornish Riviera. In 1877 the new station was described as 'neat and handsome'; there is no reason, today, to say otherwise, for it has maintained its high standards for well over a century. Despite the disappearance of the bold name boards announcing junction status, the station is still very much alive, and, 'St. Erth change for St. Ives,' has real meaning and reference.

Chapter Six
The Helston Branch

Helston is the market town and commercial centre of the Lizard peninsula. It serves a widespread and productive agricultural area and also offers access to both the beautiful riverside communities of Gweek and Helford, and the magnificent coastline for which the peninsula is famous. For just over three quarters of a century Helston was host to the railway which became a great asset to the community generally and for tourism and agriculture in particular. Passenger workings commenced on 8th May 1887 and ended on 3rd November 1962; freight trains lasted a little longer, until October 1964.

The earliest attempts to secure rail services to the town dated from the 1840s when plans were considered for a link eastward to Penryn via Gweek and Constantine. This project failed for the want of adequate support and funding, but a somewhat similar scheme was again pursued in the 1860s. Encouraged by the opening of the Cornwall Railway's line from Truro to Falmouth in August 1863, the prospectus of the Helston and Penryn Junction Railway was published locally in the autumn of 1863. The latter was intended as a broad gauge concern but it too failed to materialise despite gaining its Act of Incorporation in July 1864.

Helston eventually saw success in railway terms with the formation of the Helston Railway Company in 1879; the company being authorised by Act of Parliament in July the following year. Unlike earlier schemes, however, the new company planned their route northward from the town to join the main line from Truro to Penzance at Gwinear Road. The overall distance was 8 miles 67 chains with Messrs Maddison and Company appointed constructors.

The first effective steps towards construction followed on 22nd March 1882 with the ceremony to cut the first sod. It proved a grand occasion in view of all the previous failures; processions, an official luncheon at the Angel Hotel, treats for the local children and a generous firework display marking the event. Construction then began, but was halted in 1884 when the contractor got into difficulties. It recommenced in July 1885 with the appointment of new contractors, Messrs Lang and Son of Liskeard. Work then proceeded rapidly and was completed within two years; Colonel Rich inspecting the line on behalf of the Board of Trade on 6th May 1887. It was a steeply graded line built to standard gauge and included only one major engineering project, the Cober Viaduct, crossing the river and valley of the same name just outside Helston itself. There were originally two intermediate stations, Praze and Nancegollan; Truthwall Halt opening in July 1905. Colonel Rich was well satisfied with the standard of work on the branch, and services began three days later.

First day workings reflected the sense of occasion. The station, and the inaugural service, departing Helston at 9.40 am, were well decorated with flags and evergreen, the train running as a 'free and open service' much to the delight of the local populace. At Gwinear Road, the Chairman of the Company,

Gwinear Road soon after the opening of the Helston branch. This view looking west shows the mixed gauge on the main line and the original site of the signalbox on the 'up' platform. The train crew and station staff are posing for the photographer during a lull in traffic.
Cornwall County Museum

The busy marshalling yard east of Gwinear Road station. The number of wagons testify to the heavy goods traffic once common to West Cornwall. Gwinear Road had two signalboxes with the east box seen here to the left of the photograph alongside the main line. Access to sidings 4/5/6 was controlled by hand levers and not from the signalboxes. Note the harsh curve on the main line leading away to Camborne and the straight section on the right of the picture forming the Helston branch itself. The extensive yard seen here now belongs to the past, the site today being no more than a through road on the main line.   *P.Q. Treloar*

The view eastward from the overbridge at Gwinear Road. No. 4577 enters with a goods working off the branch which includes coaches at the rear. The fireman prepares to hand the token to the signalman whilst another locomotive waits in the sidings (beyond the train) to enter the platform and remove the stock to the sidings. Note the signalman's car parked to the right of the line and the stationmaster's house beyond the sand wagons and cattle pens.   *P.Q. Treloar*

Gwinear Road with No. 4570 having just arrived with the 5.15 p.m. from Helston on 12th September 1959. The wooden structure of the 'down' side buildings and the curvature of the main line are of note.
J.E. Bell

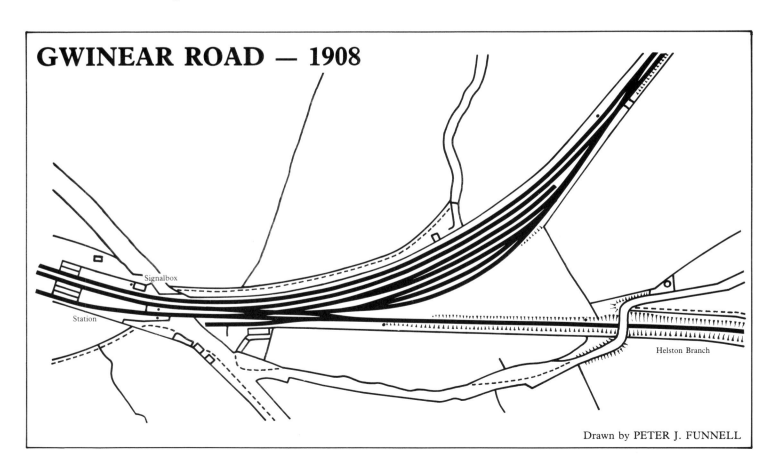

GWINEAR ROAD — 1908

Signalbox

Station

Helston Branch

Drawn by PETER J. FUNNELL

William Bickford Smith M.P. and the directors joined the train at 12.50 pm for their official journey to Helston where they were to be met by the Mayor and Corporation, members of the clergy, the Volunteer Band and the photographers. Then, prior to an official luncheon at the Angel Hotel, a further round trip was made over the branch accommodating all the appropriate local worthies.

Passenger services over the line for 1887 were as follows in the table below.

Helston	9.40	11.25	1.48	5.20	7.45
Nancegollan	9.51	11.40	1.59	5.31	7.56
Praze	9.57	11.50	2.05	5.37	8.02
Gwinear Road	10.05	12.00	2.13	5.45	8.10
Gwinear Road	10.37	12.50	2.45	7.15	8.38
Praze	10.45	1.01	2.53	7.23	8.46
Nancegollan	10.51	1.10	2.59	7.29	8.52
Helston	11.02	1.21	3.10	7.40	9.03

The opening of the branch made a great difference to Gwinear Road. Previously no more than a minor through station serving the scattered settlements of Connor Downs, Carnhell Green and the more remote Gwinear itself, it now became an important junction. The development of two busy yards east and west of the station reflected the growth of freight traffic whilst the station itself was rebuilt on a much more extensive scale. The contractor at Gwinear Road was Olver and Son of Falmouth who had been responsible for several stations on the main line and all those on the Falmouth branch.

Gwinear Road station was a wooden structure, the main buildings being on the 'down side', main line, on an island platform, the south side being used only by the branch services. The signalbox was originally at the eastern end of the 'up' platform, but was rebuilt in a similar position on the opposite platform in 1916, the platforms being extended in the previous year. West of the station, and on the north side of the line was a small goods yard with a loading platform and two roads. Perishables were loaded here, the platforms being reached by means of a long approach road north of the station.

The east yard was considerably larger, and saw extensive shunting movements which were controlled from two boxes; Gwinear Road East Box being sited at the eastern entrance to the yard, and the West Box being at the platform as mentioned. The east yard was enlarged on more than one occasion prior to World War Two. A long goods loop was opened on the 'up' (north) side of the main line, and after 1935 the GWR put in additional sidings on the south side of the yard nearest to the branch line itself. Whilst the east yard and main line curved away sharply towards the north east, the Helston branch left the station on a straight alignment almost due east. Cattle pens were provided alongside a short spur south of the branch and were reached from the Carnhell Green to Connor Downs road immediately east of the station. The road here also made it necessary to provide a level crossing which, because of its extreme width, became a recognised feature at the junction. The gates were operated from the West Box and could be something of a trial for a busy signalman during high winds, opening and closing across both the double track main line and the branch.

Shortly after leaving Gwinear Road the branch curved southward passing east of Carnhell Green on a climb to Praze, a small country station conveniently close to the village and to neighbouring Crowan. Praze just over 2¾ miles from the

No. 6845 *Paviland Grange* leaves the 'up' loop at Gwinear Road with the 1.35 p.m. broccoli and perishable working from Marazion. Gwinear Road handled extensive traffic on agricultural produce from both the surrounding area and the Helston branch. This was once a familiar scene in West Cornwall, this class of locomotive also being closely identified with the area working passenger and freight turns with ease. *P.Q. Treloar*

junction comprised a single platform west of the line, with a goods loop, ground frame, a small yard, and a water tower at the northern end of the platform. The station building, a substantial masonry structure, blended well into its pleasant wooded surroundings closeby to the Camborne-Helston road, emphasising the rural atmosphere of the branch.

Leaving Praze, the line again passed through open country this time on a falling gradient as sharp as 1 in 60 to Nancegollan, 5¼ miles from Gwinear Road. The station here was completely rebuilt and enlarged in 1937 according to the demands of traffic. Before rebuilding, the station was a modest affair with a single passenger platform and granite buildings to the west of the line. A siding also led in behind this platform from the south. Opposite the passenger platform was a goods loop and a loading platform.

Nancegollan was set amongst good agricultural land ideal for potatoes and broccoli in particular. The district was also valuable for early flowers. Well sited for consignments from the surrounding villages like Godolphin, Breage, Townshend and the fishing community of Porthleven, Nancegollan also handled considerable incoming traffic in coal and general goods for this widespread rural area.

The GWR later invested considerably in the redevelopment of Nancegollan. A totally new station and yard opened to traffic during September 1937. The main station buildings were now on the east side of the line, two platforms being provided together with a signalbox built off the north end of the opposite, 'up' platform, west of the line. Nancegollan became important therefore as a passing place on the branch. West of the station the new yard took shape. Immediately behind the passenger platforms was a goods loop, and beyond this again, serving the loop and other additional sidings, was a loading bank for the area's considerable perishable traffic. Further sidings were also provided over a period of time, these curving away westward through the yard, where they also served a goods shed.

Admiralty requirements for airfields and military establishments on the Lizard peninsula put heavy demands upon the

A branch train heading for Gwinear Road passing through the characteristically open countryside along the branch between the junction and Nancegollan. This picture shows a longer than usual train between Praze and Gwinear Road.

P.Q. Treloar

A '45XX' class locomotive shunts the yard at Nancegollen in the 1950s. Numerous wagons were needed here during the season for the broccoli and potatoe traffic coming off the branch. This yard was the result of improvements made in 1937.

P.Q. Treloar

No. 4570 stops at Nancegollan on its way to Gwinear Road on 12th September 1959. *J.E. Bell*

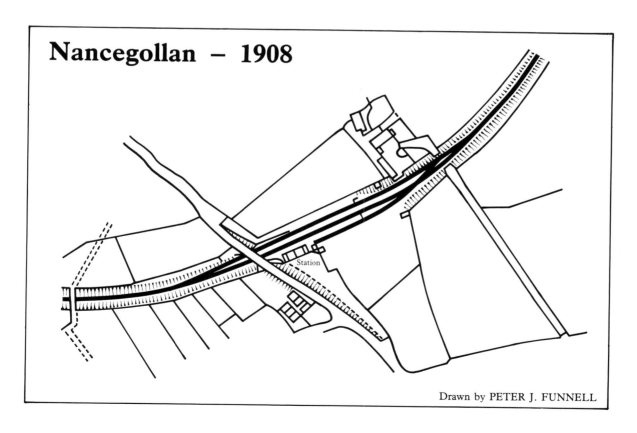

Nancegollan — 1908

Station

Drawn by PETER J. FUNNELL

branch during World War Two conveying both men and materials. This led to a need for increased siding capacity at Nancegollan and Gwinear Road, which had to be met by 1941. Military traffic in both personnel and materials continued to play an important part in the life of the line until its final closure. Many passenger trains were strengthened at peak periods of Service leave, for example, with five and six coach workings required.

Nancegollan was an attractive station set in extremely pleasant rural surroundings. A great deal of its traffic came from agricultural produce of one variety or another, whilst passengers from the neighbouring communities used the station for both their local and long distance journeys. Market day trips to Helston, Camborne or Redruth, the famous Helston Flora Day on 8th May and summer excursions to the sea at St Ives, Carbis Bay and Penzance also helped to keep the station busy. It was very much a classic GWR country station and a definitive part of the local community. This was perhaps well illustrated in smaller detail such as the series of awards it gained for its well kept station gardens emphasising the strong sense of purpose and identity that characterised the branch.

Helston, as the intended 'temporary' terminus of the line became the most southerly of all Britain's railway stations. The directors were told, however, on the opening day that if they could see their way to finding a further £100,000, the figure given for the construction of the branch, 'they should have a railway open to the Lizard, this day in two years'. The layout of the terminus showed itself as being in all respects a through station, and indeed, might possibly have been so had it not been for a significant innovation on the part of the GWR sixteen years later.

The layout at Helston comprised a single passenger platform to the west of the line with a main building of masonry housing the booking office, waiting rooms, parcels and other offices, a refreshment room, stores and toilets. At the north end of the platform was the signalbox constructed of wood with a brick base. The small locomotive depot, a sub shed of Penzance, was to the north of the signalbox. It was a single road design built of granite, with offices, a water tower and coal bunkers. The goods shed was almost opposite the main station building. It too was constructed of masonry. A single line ran through the shed continuing southward to form a loop when required. The main

A goods train near Nancegollan en route for Gwinear Road. All the stations along the line, with the exception of Truthall Halt, had busy goods yards. This scene shows No. 4552 on duty during the last years of the branch.
P.Q. Treloar

From Nancegollan southward there was more evidence of engineering works in the form of cuttings and embankments than elsewhere on the line. The gradients also intensified to 1 in 54 for a particular section down to Truthall Halt. Truthall was of spartan dimensions comprising a wooden platform strengthened by old rails and supported by timbers. A galvanised pagoda provided shelter for passengers in this lonely outpost and whilst lighting came in the form of two oil lamps. The platform only accommodated one coach but warranted no more for its purposes.

The final section of line making up some 1¾ miles from Truthall Halt to Helston itself involved severe curves on the approach to Cober Viaduct and a short climb to reach the terminus. Before describing the latter, however, the Cober Viaduct deserves some consideration. It constituted the heaviest engineering feature on the branch, being 373 yards long with six arches. Quarried from granite obtained nearby, the viaduct stood 90 feet high and was completed at a cost of £6,000.

loop for run-round purposes on the passenger trains was between the goods shed and the branch platform. The layout also provided for two lengthy sidings to the south of the station beyond the run-round loop. A carriage shed was also provided there at the extreme end of the line. On the east side of the goods yard was a loading platform served by a straight single road siding; cattle pens being provided there. Beyond the goods platform was a slaughter house and stable buildings. The layout at Helston allowed for goods and passenger facilities to be kept reasonably separate, each having its own approach road and working area to the east and west of the site respectively.

The opening of the branch certainly encouraged local agriculture and with direct access to all parts of the railway system, Helston's trade both inward and outward improved. The town's status as a market centre was therefore much enhanced. Although the railway arrived somewhat later than at neighbouring Falmouth or Penzance to the east and west, its presence was imperative in commercial development. The railway was

Helston terminus in the earlier years of the line. The solid granite station building, GWR poster, advertisements and milk churns are all prominent here. The locomotive shed can be seen in the distance, with the signalbox sited at the end of the platform. The branch line curves away to the right under the bridge.

Cornwall County Museum

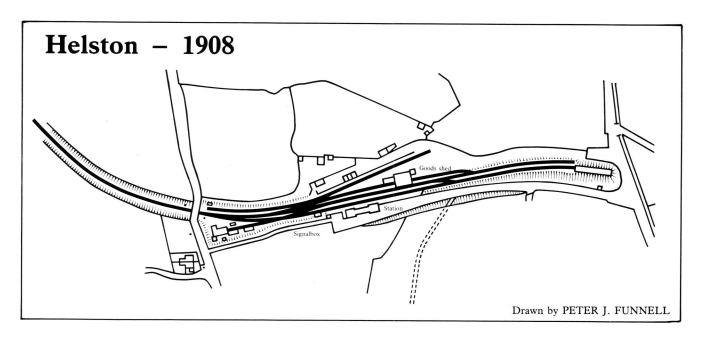

Helston — 1908

Goods shed

Station

Signalbox

Drawn by PETER J. FUNNELL

No. 4570 at Helston after arriving with the 4.35 p.m. from Gwinear Road on 12th September 1959. *J.E. Bell*

'4500' class No. 4570 leaving Helston for Gwinear Road in the final years of the branch service. The station building, goods shed and sidings are seen in the background. Alongside the train is the loading chute for stone traffic installed during the 1950s. *P.Q. Treloar*

without doubt the great symbol of progress for the nineteenth century as expressed locally in the banners and commemorations displayed at the cutting of the first sod. 'Perseverance Ensures Success' and Railways and Increase Trade' were clear statements of hope and regard for the future of the town; a future which the people believed with all sincerity could only lie with the railway. An indication of the progressive mood at Helston during that time came with the reorganisation and development of the Helston Gas Company. Plans were put forward to extend and improve gas supplies with new and heavier pipes for distribution. The station, on the east side of the town, was given something of a priority with the intention to provide gas lighting for the main building, platform and the approach road. It was considered essential to rid the station of oil lamps thereby improving its image and its efficiency. The work began in the Autumn of 1887. All in and outgoing mail for the Helston district, other than the first morning delivery, was also transferred to rail by the Autumn of 1887. Previously it had travelled via Penryn.

Soon after opening, the GWR revealed its pleasure at developments on the line, the Company being 'openly surprised at the largeness of goods traffic'. Tourism was also set to develop within the area. The attractions of the Lizard peninsula had much to offer the visitor, particularly those of affluent means. By the turn of the century there were several large and imposing hotels along the coastline with the GWR for its part being only too pleased to promote its services to this distinguished part of Britain. All the delights of the Helford River and attractive fishing villages such as Mullion Cove and Coverack for example were now much more accessible adding further appeal to the idea of a Cornish Riviera. The Great Western had, in fact, operated the services over the line since its opening, but in 1898 the Helston Railway Company was dissolved making the branch a full and valuable possession of the GWR.

A decisive improvement to services came in August 1903 when the Great Western introduced its first omnibus operating from Helston to the Lizard. Two 16 horse power Milnes Daimler vehicles fitted with open wagonette bodies and roof canopy worked the 11 mile route, taking one hour to cover the journey. The first buses ran on 17th August with three services each day.

Considerations for further rail extensions into the Lizard peninsula were abandoned with the introduction of the omnibuses. It had been hoped to extend the railway to the Lizard in the last years of the nineteenth century along with other schemes to win Light Railway Orders in West Cornwall. The timetable for the branch in 1909 also showed that the omnibuses operated all Sunday services, there being no trains. Journey times from Gwinear Road to the terminus with only one intermediate call at Nancegollan was given as 70 minutes. Weekday services over the branch at that time consisted of nine trains in each direction.

Exactly half a century later there were little more than slight changes in journey times although there were more trains on Summer Saturdays in 1959. Rapid change took place in the following three years however. Notice of closure was given for early November 1962 and, accordingly on Saturday 3rd November passenger services ceased, despite spirited opposition locally. Officially, the branch closed on 5th November, but as there was no Sunday service for 4th November the last ran on the Saturday night, this being the connecting service for the 1.30 pm departure from Paddington to Penzance. It arrived at Helston at 10.00 pm met by a considerable number of people anxious to witness the event. Steam had disappeared completely from the branch by this time, Penzance locomotive depot closing to steam in September 1962. The last passenger train to Helston was hauled by D 6312 a North British hydraulic locomotive later listed as Class 22. Freight traffic continued until 4th October 1964. On the following day, 5th October 1964, Gwinear Road and several other main line stations closed. Without the branch, Gwinear Road served no real purpose and, without the freight traffic generated locally, the large yard there also came under sentence.

Precious little of the line remains today. Gwinear Road, other than as a through road on the main line, is a wilderness and the alignment of the branch has disappeared in field reclamation. None of the stations survive on the branch itself; indeed, Nancegollan is now the site of a factory, and Helston, that of a housing estate. The Cober Viaduct remains intact, but now there is little else to see of what was once a busy, if somewhat modest, country branch line.

FULL SUMMER SERVICE 1959

	S	E	S		S	S			E	S		
Helston	5.45	7.45	7.45	9.45	10.20	11.50	1.15	3.20	4.10	4.35	7.00	8.37
Truthall Plat	—	7.51	—	—	—	—	—	3.27	4.17	4.41	7.06	8.43
Nancegollan	—	7.58	7.58	9.56	10.31	12.02	1.25	3.34	4.25	4.48	7.12	8.49
Praze	—	8.04	8.04	10.02	10.37	12.08	1.31	3.40	4.31	4.54	7.19	8.56
Gwinear Road	6.10	8.12	8.12	10.10	10.45	12.15	1.40	3.47	4.38	5.05	7.27	9.04

	S			S	E	S	S	S		E	S	E	S	S			E	S
Gwinear Road	6.15	7.30	8.35	10.15	10.50	11.05	12.37	1.48	2.25	3.55	4.12	4.30	5.00	5.24	6.55	7.50	9.20	9.30
Praze	6.23	7.40	8.42	10.23	10.58	11.13	12.44	1.56	2.32	4.02	4.19	4.40	5.08	5.32	7.03	7.58	9.28	9.38
Nancegollan	6.29	8.00	8.48	10.30	11.04	11.19	12.50	2.02	2.39	4.08	4.26	4.50	5.15	5.39	7.13	8.04	9.34	9.44
Truthall Plat	—	—	8.54	10.36	11.10	11.25	12.56	—	2.45	4.14	4.32	—	5.21	5.45	—	—	9.40	9.50
Helston	6.40	8.20	9.00	10.44	11.15	11.30	1.02	2.12	2.51	4.20	4.38	5.01	5.27	5.50	7.25	8.14	9.45	9.55

E — Except Saturdays
S — Saturdays Only
Connecting Bus Service Between Helston Station, The Lizard and Mullion Cove. Not Shown Here.

Chapter Seven
Agricultural Traffic

The genial climate of West Cornwall that proved such an attraction for visitors and residents alike, was also the vital factor in the development of local agriculture. Market Gardening and dairying flourished with the help of the railway, and districts such as the famous 'Golden Mile', between the villages of Gulval and Ludgvan, a short distance east of Penzance, became well known for the quality of their produce.

Rail facilities for the earliest years at Penzance have already been described elsewhere, and it was clear that with the heavy demand for market-garden produce, new sidings at Ponsandane and Marazion were soon required. *The West Briton* provided details of consignments over the period 1867-1870:

'The annual average despatch of early potatoes from Penzance for the past four seasons is 2,337 tons, and of broccoli, 2,627 tons. The largest total of potatoes was in 1863 when 3,146 tons were despatched, and of broccoli in 1868 when the quantity was 3,571 tons.'

This reflected good business to the extent that in just two days, in June 1870, 450 tons of potatoes left Penzance and Marazion.

There were positive developments for trade during 1871. In June a delightfully picturesque description was offered of the scene at Penzance:

'At Penzance Railway Station there has been 'a roaring trade' doing for the past fortnight . . . Fish baskets are seen piled in immense heaps, also endless hampers of potatoes, and huge broad gauge engines puffing and snorting to and fro pulling long lines of trucks all crammed with produce of the west.'

A noteworthy consignment from the parishes of Madron, Ludgvan and Gulval and destined for the North Midlands markets and Lancashire, was that of 120 tons of gooseberries and quantities of local currants. Also that month a farm at Ludgvan, sent 72 baskets of strawberries on the Mail train to London, and it was reported that 'a great many special trains are despatched in the course of the day direct through to Bristol and London'. The telegraph was considered vital in view of the trade from agriculture and fisheries. Open day and night, there was a call for an exclusive wire direct from West Cornwall to London to cope with the demand from this office.

Fruit was a welcome addition to that of vegetables, but in 1875 *The West Briton* was also reporting on the progress of dairying:

'Dairy farming is now being carried on, on a greatly increased scale in the West of Cornwall. On Thursday last no less than six tons of fresh butter was sent off from Penzance railway station to diverse parts of the kingdom. On the previous Thursday about six tons were also transmitted in the same way. In fact, from five to seven tons are being sent away every week from this one station. The principal towns to which it is consigned are Dudley, Birmingham, Sheffield, Bristol and London. One buyer alone in Penzance market last Thursday bought half a ton: The present price of butter in Cornish markets is 1s. to 1s. 1d. per lb. Six tons at this rate would realise £672. Fancy between £4,000 and £5,000 worth of fresh butter being sent away from one station in about a month. Large quantities are also sent away from Truro and other Cornish stations.'

Harvesting potatoes near St Buryan on the Lands End peninsula. The photograph dates from the late 1870s. Unlike today, this crop would undoubtedly have been bound for Penzance and the railway station for consignment eastward.

Cornwall County Museum

WEST CORNWALL RAILWAY.

ON AND AFTER JANUARY THE SECOND, 1860,

BROCOLI AND NEW POTATOES

Will be conveyed from PENZANCE or ~~~~~ to the following Stations, viz.:—

	BY GOODS TRAIN.				BY PASSENGER TRAIN, In limited quantities, subject to the convenience of the Company.			
	Owner's Risk.		Company's Risk.		Owner's Risk.		Company's Risk.	
	Brocoli, per ton.	Potatoes, per ton.	Brocoli, per ton.	Potatoes, per ton.	Brocoli, per ton.	Potatoes, per ton.	Brocoli, per ton.	Potatoes, per ton.
PADDINGTON	55s.	50s.	80s.	80s.	80s.	80s.	Parcel Rates.	Parcel Rates.
BATH	35s.	35s.	60s.	60s.	65s.	65s.	do.	do.
BRISTOL	30s.	30s.	55s.	55s.	60s.	65s.	do.	do.
EXETER	25s.	25s.	35s.	35s.	—	—	do.	do.
PLYMOUTH	15s.	15s.	25s.	25s.	—	—	do.	do.

Brocoli and New Potatoes intended to be forwarded by Goods Train must be brought to the Stations not later than 3.30 p.m. to ensure their being dispatched on the same day. The above charges are exclusive of collection or delivery.

(BY ORDER),

C. P. CHARLTON, Secretary.

Penzance, December 31st, 1859.

One of the earliest known references to perishable traffic by rail in West Cornwall.

By the close of the decade the Great Western enjoyed very positive returns from West Cornwall's potato traffic. £20,000 was earned by the beginning of August for the 1879 season. The scene in July that year was encouraging: 'The export last week contrary to expectation is estimated to exceed that of the preceeding which was 2,000 tons. Every day a constant stream of carts was seen moving railway-ward to the Gulval sidings. Four and five trains a day of some 16 to 20 trucks were sent off. Some days 600 tons have left from Gulval siding alone.'

A great deal of the perishable traffic described here originated in the important agricultural parishes of Gulval and Ludgvan, being neighbouring districts within easy reach of the railway. As already indicated they were blessed with some of the very finest soils in Cornwall and were, therefore, busy places reflecting high levels of employment. In considering the influence of agricultural traffic for the railway, it would also be something of an insight locally to trace aspects of life of the rural community that supplied the goods.

Rural districts and their circumstances such as those at Gulval should form an integral part of the railway story overall. In 1867 Gulval parish had a population of 1,742 and an overall acreage recorded at 4,357. 'The Royal Commission on the Employment of Children, Young Persons and Women in Agriculture 1867-68' gives a detailed picture of the people who worked this land.

According to the commission, Gulval had mixed cultivation with 400 women, young persons and children employed. Those at work ranged in age from 7 to 70 years working from 8 am to 6 pm, the men's employment obviously covering longer hours. In their evidence to the commission, the three cases set out below give good example of life and work at Gulval.

The first, William Rowe, aged 7, was said to have been working, 'putting down potatoes for two years for his father who holds four fields – two in grass for cows, two in gardens (fields). The boy looks after the cow, when he cannot, his sister does, who is nine years of age. He is very irregular in his attendance at school'.

Both parents and employers were frequently responsible for keeping their children away from the village school: in this case the parent was the employer, and as the next extract also shows child labour was commonplace.

The second example is that of Ellen Pierce, aged 11:

'I have been out pulling radishes at 7 pence (3p) a day on hours of work from 8 am to 6 pm. I go home to dinner at 12 o'clock and begin again at 1 pm. Men, women, boys and girls all worked together potatoing; we were seven girls, five boys, three women and one man to fill in the drills (planting); the women get 10d a day.
The older girls go away early from the morning school to cook or carry dinner for their mothers in the gardens. My aunt works in the gardens (fields), gets 5 or 6 shillings a week. 10d a day is the wage for day work... In my cottage we have one kitchen, one bedroom, and a dairy where my mother, aunt, grandmother and myself live together.'

Finally the evidence of a Mr Thomas, a holder of market gardens at Gulval:

'The garden work is mostly taken by the piece; fruit picking by the gallon. A man's wages are 2 shillings a day at the lowest; a steady man gets 13 shillings to 15 shillings a week. Women get 10d to 1 shilling a day. Girls begin work at the age of 9 or 10 years and get 6d a day ... Women can earn by piecework a day and a half's wages in the day. I think it would be just to keep boys from work until they were 10 years of age, such a limit would not inflict any injury on the employer but might possibly do so to the labourers' families.

In the potatoe season a man's wages are £1 a week mostly all money – few give drink. The best land is let at £10 an acre. My holding varies from £4 to £10 a year. The labourers do not save much, they lose a good many day's work and the women have to work hard.'

If nothing else, these extracts illustrate the gulf that existed between the growing tourist market for the middle and upper classes in West Cornwall and the lives of many of the local people, whose horizons were strictly limited, not least by financial hardship. Despite the familiar hardships for agricultural workers, the community was sustained through its alliance with the railway ensuring valuable markets in other parts of the country. The prosperity built around local agriculture was vitally important to the district and stood in sharp contrast with certain other parts of Britain where the rural economy had suffered extensively from foreign competition. Encouraged by the growth of rail services, West Cornwall adapted its agriculture to the changing demands of the market place, concentrating on the supply of a range of perishable crops and dairy products. West Cornwall, of course, was but one of many parts of Britain that showed a flexible approach to the rural economy. It differed from other such areas like the Vale of Evesham, Lincolnshire or Cheshire in its famous mild climate allowing valuable early crops to reach the markets well ahead of the larger rivals. The railway's contribution was invaluable here.

Despite such success, the years in the immediate future brought dispute over the question of traffic rates, and the growth of competition from steamships offering more attractive rates. Indeed, by 1885 the GWR rates were described locally as, 'prohibitive to a serious degree', and regular services supplying Liverpool and the north-west were organised by sea. Since 1882 two steamships had been operating out of Penzance on this service, carrying over 5,000 tons in the four-year period. The LSWR attracted traffic by operating a steamer from West Cornwall to Devonport, where it linked with its own rail network. A steamship service for vegetable traffic, from Penzance to Avonmouth was also introduced in 1889 in conjunction with the Midland Railway. The Great Western responded with the provision of an express goods for broccoli traffic, but its rates were considerably higher.

A conflict of interest at this particular time was singularly unfortunate for the GWR as by 1865 it was estimated that there were 1,000 acres of broccoli under cultivation in the Penzance district. In the same year, the Isles of Scilly sent across its largest ever consignment of potatoes to the mainland, destined for London and the Midland Counties, and amounting to 1,600 baskets. The flower industry was developing rapidly and the market for anemones, daffodils, violets and narcissus blooms was established, providing by the turn of the century, shipments from the Scillies alone of 25 to 50 tons on frequent occasions. The LSWR also fought for their share of this traffic, and in particular instances sailing vessels were chartered to take consignments direct from the Isles of Scilly to Plymouth in order to meet the South Western Railway. Tugs were also employed when winds were contrary to ensure efficient deliveries. In three weeks to the beginning of May 1898, the GWR lost £1,700 in revenue from flower traffic passing to their rival, giving some indication of the overall scale and potential for business. From one day's trade alone, in March 1896, 5,605 crates of broccoli left West Cornwall by rail.

As late as 1891, however, many traders in West Cornwall seriously considered the possibility of some direct railway competition through the active presence of the LSWR at Penzance. They were quite specific about this:

'In regard to the present railway service and rates it be deemed a County object of the first importance to promote the extension of the London and South Western Railway westward until it reaches Penzance, on the one hand, and Falmouth on the other.'

Whatever their actual prospects, the sentiments behind these aspirations were real enough, but developments soon after the turn of the century revealed a decidedly new direction of thought on the part of the railway companies themselves.

In January 1907, *The Cornishman* newspaper carried the following report:

'We are informed that it is the intention of the great companies to divide up the kingdom into 'spheres of influence' in which each company will have practically uncontrolled sway, and that one of the first manifestations of this policy will be found to be the closing of various branch offices now maintained by other companies in those areas.'

The report ended with the view that such developments could only be seen as matters for 'the gravest concern on the part of traders and the general public'. Without doubt, it was an approach that ran counter to the whole pattern of trade as it existed at that time, but hindsight shows that this particular period, leading to the Railway Grouping of 1923, was decisive in shaping the future pattern of railway working. The concept of 'spheres of influence', considered in 1907, was later formulated into definite policy under the Railways Act of 1921. It was the long-term and inevitable outcome of the experience of the First World War together with the recognition by the railway companies themselves, that extensive efforts at competition were frequently wasteful of money and resources. The logic of events in these early and formative years of the present century, therefore, brought the interests of both the community in West Cornwall and those of the GWR into sharp focus.

In its efforts to eliminate the more negative elements of competition the government legislation, through the Railways Act and the Grouping, acknowledged the GWR as the predominant interest in Cornwall, thereby setting the terms of reference for future development. Given its overall performance within the county, the Company was well placed to encourage business, drawing on experience and a proven record of achievement in the past.

Relations between the local community of West Cornwall and the GWR were marked by positive mutual regard during the inter-war era, and considerable progress was achieved, to the extent that the Penzance Chamber of Commerce, early in 1936, could claim: 'Those of us who are in a position to know, realise the immense value of the work of the Great Western Railway in helping the trade and commerce of the county'.

Government policy towards agriculture during the First World War had illustrated the way in which production could be stimulated by intervention on behalf of the industry. The successful increases in crop levels by means of careful regulation were not, however, pursued in the years immediately after the war, despite the initial intention to do so; economic factors were said to have cautioned against this. In the decade leading to the outbreak of the Second World War the situation was somewhat different.

As early as 1895, the Market Gardeners' Compensation Act had helped to reduce the risks for tenants investing in their property, providing an early stimulus to increased production. More widespread and detailed assistance came later. In 1928, for example, agricultural land was de-rated, thereby relieving some of the burdens on costs, and soon after this the railways also

Above: No. 4566 shunting cattle wagons used for the broccoli and potato traffic at Marazion Yard. 11th May 1959.   *M. Mensing*

Left: Loading flowers at Penzance during the early 1950s. West Cornwall and the Isles of Scilly were able to provide large consignments of early season flowers for markets all over Britain.
Cornwall County Museum

Below: Loading broccoli on the goods platforms at Marazion in 1959. The yard was worked to capacity with such traffic when required as Marazion served an extensive and rich agricultural area. Sidings were first provided here in West Cornwall Railway days, giving almost a century of continuous working reaching its peak in the early years of nationalisation.   *P.Q. Treloar*

Just over a century after through rail traffic was first made possible, No. 6805 *Broughton Grange* typifies the presence of the GWR and its successor, the Western Region, before the wide sweeping changes of the 1960s. The photograph, dated 7th April 1960, shows a fitted freight climbing eastward at Rospeath, between Marazion and St Erth.   *P.Q. Treloar*

received similar help when their rates were cut. Lower rates for the railways also helped agriculture of course, in as far as they were able to pass on savings in the form of lower charges. The Ministry of Agriculture also obtained the new variety of 'Roscoff' seed of broccoli for the 1929 season. This was distributed to growers locally, by Cornwall County Council and resulted in significant crop increases, estimated at 150% on the previous year. New wooden crates were also introduced to improve packaging; these replacing the old wicker and net baskets, on a non returnable basis.

Marketing Boards for commodities such as potatoes and milk followed in 1931 and 1933. Five dairies were in production by the turn of the century in the Lands End peninsula, and in 1935 a new creamery was developed at St. Erth alongside the railway yard. The marketing boards were responsible for valuable increase in production, to the mutual satisfaction of the community and the railway. Import duties to regulate competition from Europe were introduced from 1931 (The Horticultural Products Act) with some positive results for flower and vegetable traffic.

By 1936 flower and broccoli traffic had made particular progress. The local acreage of anemones had recently risen from fifty to five hundred acres, and the contribution of the railway was acknowledged specifically, in this case. In tribute to the

enterprise of the railway, the Penzance Chamber of Commerce stated: Had it not been for the GWR, research (the cultivation of anemones) would not have taken place in this county'. The Company had in fact, provided a subsidy of £250 on an annual basis for a three year period in order to further research. Just over 2,000 tons of flowers were handled by the GWR at Penzance in 1937, with 2,432 tons in the previous year. Broccoli traffic had also increased positively, from a very respectable figure of 31,495 tons in 1936, to 35,490 tons in 1937. Prior to this, for example, in January 1935, 73 special trains left the Penzance district in the course of one week, conveying heavy consignments of broccoli. It was recorded that for the previous year only one special train left during the corresponding period on account of poor weather conditions. General traffic handling also showed an increase of 7,000 tons to a figure of 55,347 tons for 1937. Great Western investment in the new goods depot at Ponsandane that particular year was well placed.

With the outbreak of war in 1939, West Cornwall was also in a strong position to contribute effectively to the need for increased levels of food production required under the emergency arrangements. The value of recent investment in the district was then put to its most severe test demonstrating the full extent of the progress and achievement accomplished in the final years of peace.

Chapter Eight
The Fishing Trade

The railway had a decisive effect on the growth and structure of the fishing industry in Cornwall. Newlyn, in particular, was developed over the second half of the nineteenth century to become the premier Cornish fishing port and a focal point for the industry in the West Country generally. Close proximity to the lucrative fishing grounds of West Cornwall made Newlyn a prime location for growth. The railway made it possible to exploit ready markets, particularly for fresh mackerel, in London, the Midlands and the North in a manner and scale that was without precedent. Provisions for rapid and regularised transit of fish stocks also resulted in the appearance of visiting fleets from Lowestoft and the East Coast attracted by the prospects of valuable profits from the catch.

An early indication of the value of railway links for trade is seen in the consignment, in August 1861, of 1,063 tons of fish, 1,787 tons of potatoes and 867 tons of broccoli from Penzance reflecting very positively on the potential for traffic. By April 1868 *The West Briton* was recording considerable progress:

'On Thursday night the Mounts Bay fishery was a splendid success. The first boats arrived at Newlyn at eight and nine o'clock Friday morning, and the good nights work was soon apparent. All day long the fish were being rapidly carted from Newlyn to Penzance and kept the roads, streets and the railway station very busy. The total catch brought in and despatched from Penzance was 115 tons. No less than five thousand baskets of fish were rapidly despatched by three specials, and the Mail train on Friday; and mackerel which that morning swam in shoals seven or eight miles south-west of the dreaded Wolf Rock were sold in Billingsgate early on Saturday morning. On the same day 20 tons were sent from Hayle, making the total about 325,000 fish for the night's catch.'

The report reveals a particular fascination for time, speed, and organisation seen in the sharp contrast between 'the dreaded Wolf Rock' and Billingsgate Market. Shortly before this, in November 1866, the broad gauge was extended over the West Cornwall Railway from Truro to Penzance, establishing through

A Lowestoft trawler taking on coal at Newlyn's North Pier during the interwar years. The extensive fish market built after World War One can be seen in the background.
Cornwall County Museum

traffic. The break in gauge at Truro had resulted in a certain amount of lost revenue. During August 1863 the Cornwall Railway opened to Falmouth, thereby avoiding Penzance, and the expensive and time consuming process of transfer at Truro. By the end of the decade there was further progress.

In April 1869 the West Cornwall Steamship Company purchased a 189 ton steamer named *Rover* for work on the fishing grounds about West Cornwall. This vessel, originating from Liverpool, was capable of carrying 100 tons of fish and could act as a valuable means of transport, picking up from ships still at sea, fetching fish consignments from the Isles of Scilly on a daily basis, and acting as a tug for becalmed boats needing to be moved to or from the fishing grounds. The steamship obviously improved deliveries, working in conjunction with the railway to meet the schedule for the Mail train, or to provide a loading of fifteen tons which was the necessary requirement for a 'special' train. With the direct assistance of *Rover*, one outstanding double-headed fish 'special' of sixty tons left Penzance in May 1869, whilst the full week ending the 21 May 1869 saw some 132 tons of fish pass through Penzance station.

Traffic levels by this time represented a considerable attraction to the rival London and South Western Railway. Stimulated by criticisms of the current arrangements, the LSWR entered the market in March 1871, bringing, for many, an element of welcome competition. Earlier, in April 1870, the St. Ives fishery voiced open dissatisfaction with services. It was maintained: 'If a steamer was on the line from Bideford, then the South Western Company would get the traffic'. In view of the fact that in one week of May in that year fish traffic brought returns of some £2,400, loss of revenue to new rivals would be a serious matter. The new service for March 1871 was based around the activities of the West Cornwall Fishing Steam Company, formed to carry large fish consignments by steamer to railheads at Exmouth and Bideford. Monopolies of trade were rarely received very favourably and the new service promised vigorous competition and the advantages that accompanies an enterprise 'under one management'. The promoters of this new initiative expressed their views in forthright terms:

'The greatest inconvenience has frequently seen experienced, and heavy losses have been sustained by consignors of fish, vegetables and various perishable articles . . . in consequence of there being but one route available for conveyance. . . . In anticipation of the approaching mackerel season, it has been determined to engage a fast steamboat to run in connection with this Railway Company between St. Ives and Bideford, or Penzance and Exmouth according to the requirements of trade. The London & South Western Railway Company will deliver the fish at a most reasonable rate into Billingsgate market by special and other trains, and, 'the whole line to London being under one management', there will be no stoppage or delays. The fish will be delivered much cheaper than at present.'

In the summer of 1876 the mayor of Penzance personally travelled to Plymouth to urge representations on the LSWR to extend their services westward, and, to make some immediate provision for steamer facilities to cover a Penzance to Devonport sailing on a regular basis. The War Office and the Admiralty had earlier made their own particular representations to the LSWR to complete their line westward to Lydford so that stores 'may go from Portsmouth to Plymouth without break of gauge'.

When the GWR assumed its effective control over the entire route to the west, however, services were improved. In that particular year, (1876), new goods shed facilities offering modern covered accommodation were provided at Penzance station. In July 1879, *The West Briton* sounded a hopeful note on the provision of the third rail and mixed gauge working:

'It is stated on good authority that the South Devon and Cornwall sections of the GWR are to have the third rail laid. Decision has been arrived at in connection with the considerations affecting the heavy consignments of potatoes, fish and broccoli from the west.'

The undoubted improvement never actually materialised, but a lot was achieved in 1879. *The West Briton* provided the details:

'No less than four long fish trains passed over the Cornwall lines on Friday in addition to some trucks being attached to the Mail. It is calculated that about as many fish have already gone over the line as during the whole of last season. (5 May 1879).'

In April it had been announced that an extra fish train was to run on a schedule 3-15 minutes ahead of the Mail at 3.15 and, if necessary, with a catch giving a further load of ten tons, another 'special' would depart, this time at 5 p.m. Arrangements allowed for special trains to be organised at a mere three hours notice provided the load was a minimum of twenty tons, the rate for London being set at £4 per ton. A most positive statement appeared in May:

'Not only do West Cornwall Steamship Company boats help to stimulate the fishery and ensure good prices, but the railways pay more attention than ever to the swifter and cheaper conveyance of the mackerel. Never have the train arrangements been so good. The price per ton, once over £7.10s. is reduced to £4.10s. and telegraphic word from Scilly of quantities puts Mr. J.G. Bone, the alert Station Master, and Mr. Ivy, the local head of the Locomotive Department, on the que-vive, so that special train may hurry the fish away. The heaviest day we have seen this season saw the despatch of nearly 200 tons; the heaviest week, 800 tons. We hope for many, very many days yet when 100 tons may be carried.

Progress also meant the provision of efficient rolling stock. From 1878 new vehicles appeared, incorporating the frames of old six-wheeled coaches and were frequently worked in the formation of passenger trains. The 1880s saw further improvements when new stock was built comprising flat wooden wagon bodies with a central guard's compartment, oil axles boxes and vacuum brakes. The emphasis here was with fast and reliable performances up to the standard of commendable passenger workings.

Ironically, the GWR was set to achieve its best performance on a fish train in Cornwall at a time when the Company was in considerable dispute with the fisheries over traffic rates. In May 1888 a double-headed special of 80 tons completed the run to Plymouth in 3 hours 6 minutes including two stops, at Truro and Lostwithiel, for water, this being the fastest performance to date, given the loadings involved. In June of the same year the Newlyn branch of the National Sea Fisheries Protection Association appealed to the GWR to reduce rates. For their part, the railway was prepared to carry fish on Saturdays at a reduced rate of 10s. per ton as steamers worked by Bazeley and Son of Penzance shipped fish from Newlyn on that day. Bedford Bolitho MP took the fishermen's case to the House of Commons, but in the meantime advised fishermen to 'show their appreciation of the enterprise of Messrs Bazeley and Son, and retaliate on the railway company by making as much use of the steamers as possible'. Five years earlier a leading article in *The Cornishman* expressed anger over high rates of carriage, the GWR accused of 'making a greedy hole in the poor fisherman's pocket'. Even worse:

'It would be useless to appeal to the better feelings of a railway company for they appear to have none; but such egregious extortion as we find here (Rates at £5 per ton as against ordinary goods at 15s. 11d.) is certainly unwarrantable, and is only maintained by the virtue of the monopoly which the GWR so securely enjoys in this part of the country.'

The International Fisheries Exhibition held in London in 1883 helped promote closer links between West Cornwall and fishing interests elsewhere, and gave the GWR an opportunity to stress its contribution to the industry. Special fares to 'authenticated Cornish fishermen and fisherwomen and curers of fish' were made available on a third-class excursion ticket valid for a month for all services apart from the 11.15 a.m. departure from Penzance, and the 11.45 a.m. from Paddington.

Progress and increased prosperity was most clearly indicated in the major programme of development at Newlyn itself. This was the legacy of the 1880s when a modern port enclosing some 40 acres of tidal waters was constructed. The South Pier, developed from 1885, was 700 feet long when completed, with a lighthouse to protect shipping. This South Pier involved costs of £20,000 whilst in 1888 a North Pier was built and later extended, in 1894, to reach 1,760 feet at a cost of £32,000 overall. These extensive improvements together with production from local ice-works and large scale imports of ice from Norway show that fishing interests at Newlyn were operating on an extensive scale. The Statistical Tables for the Sea Fisheries of the United Kingdom, 1891-1895 reflect this expansion. The following official figures relate to the *total* catches for Newlyn and St. Ives, as the main ports of West Cornwall.

	1891	**1892**	**1893**	**1894**	**1895**
Penzance/Newlyn	4158 tons	5364	5526	6300	6720
St. Ives	5696 tons	5068	4769	3626	3891

The total value of the Penzance and Newlyn fishery for 1895 was £99,187. At St. Ives the total was £23,876 with Mevagissey, the nearest rival, at £10,742.

Events in May 1896, however, revealed that progress did not necessarily make for cordial relations, particularly when commercial interests came into direct conflict with local traditions. The East Coast fleets, anxious to take full advantage of the markets made it their business to begin fishing on Sundays and to land and dispose of their catch for a market on Mondays. This, however, ran counter to Cornish practices where fishing on the Sabbath was forbidden, and serious disorder followed when Lowestoft crews attempted to land their catch from a weekend sailing in mid May. The Newlyn men with the support of crews from St. Ives opposed this move violently, and in force. Such was the scale and intensity of the conflict, that, together with a considerable police presence, a 'special' train conveying four field training companies of 'The Second Berkshire Regiment' numbering between 200-300 men was despatched to Penzance. A large crowd had gathered in the precincts of the station having heard of the troop train but only the Justices and other officials were allowed inside. The troops disembarked and marched across the quay and the promenade to a temporary barracks immediately west of the promenade. Amidst continuing trouble the troops occupied the South Pier to protect the East Coast fishermen from further damage whilst the torpedo destroyer *Ferret* steamed into the Bay and anchored offshore. The Lowestoft crews were persuaded to sail and to work out of Penzance in future as the community there was more sympathetic. In a statement, the Newlyn men declared:

'We are true Cornishmen, fighting for truth, honesty and Christianity; we will have our Sundays honoured – and if the Lowestoft men are not allowed to bring in fish on Mondays we shall have a better price on Tuesdays.'

An unsuccessful appeal was made by Newlyn Committee to the Home Secretary on behalf of the local community, and questions were put to the Home Secretary and the Attorney General in the House of Commons on 1 June in support of the East Coast men generally. Compensation of a figure between £600 and £700 followed in January 1897.

Immediately before the turn of the century, in 1899, *The West Briton* drew attention to a remarkable week's fishing linked to Newlyn. The report allows for a fascinating glimpse into the work of the community and, significantly, includes the railway:

'During the past week it is computed that more than a million mackerel were landed and despatched from Newlyn. This means that several hundred fishermen secure the fish anywhere between sixty and seventy miles from the land. Two to three hundred craft are involved in the capture. Perhaps three hundred miles of net were shot for that purpose. Secondly, it calls for the aid of an army of workers on the shore and the baggage train of the brigade in the shape of horses, wagons, lorries, a flotilla of row boats, many scores of packers, ice preparers and odd hands, scores of tons of ice used for keeping the fish cool, scores of tons of straw and paper used for packing – perhaps 20,000 boxes laden and sent up the line.'

Unlike many Cornish fishing ports, Newlyn was in a strong position to contend with demands of the twentieth century. As a result of its prime position for the fishing grounds, its excellent harbour amenities and the close proximity of a main-line railway, Newlyn continued to grow in prosperity unlike many other traditional fishing centres that experienced a visible decline. Increasingly, during the course of the present century, Cornish fishing ports have turned to tourism and their basic economy and character has, manifestly, been transformed. This has never been the case at Newlyn. From a survey of Devon and Cornwall's ports in the inter-war years, Newlyn's position was seen to be secure. The figures refer to the percentage of the total catch for the four leading fishing ports, in 1919 and 1938.

	1919	**1938**
Plymouth	19%	11%
Brixham	18%	15%
Newlyn	31%	57%
St. Ives	20%	3%

St. Ives had clearly suffered the heaviest decline but, by 1938, had achieved a new basis for prosperity as a GWR holiday resort.

As the focal point of fishing operations in the West Country, however, Newlyn was set to receive further significant investment shortly after World War One, when £20,000 was spent on a new covered fish market, sales offices and a new road scheme to link both piers along the shore. As always, the GWR was mindful of the importance of Newlyn as a source of highly lucrative traffic, and whilst it could not compare, for example, with the scale of development carried out by the Manchester Sheffield and Lincolnshire Railway at Grimsby, the Great Western's particular contribution to the overall success of Newlyn was considerable.

ST. IVES.

Very Ancient and interesting Borough.

Lovely Climate.   Bracing, with very slight variation
- - of temperature. - -

CHARMING SCENERY.   BEAUTIFUL BEACHES.

. . FIRST-CLASS . .
HOTELS AND BOARDING HOUSES.

Head-quarters of the Pilchard Seine Fishery.

. . Ten Minutes by Rail . .
from the celebrated West Cornwall Golf Links.

SEA FISHING. - *BOATING.*

SAFE BATHING.

COACHING EXCURSIONS to —

ST. MICHAEL'S MOUNT.	ZENNOR.
GURNARD'S HEAD.	PRUSSIA COVE.
LAND'S END.	THE LIZARD & KYNANCE.

and to other places of interest.

A page advertisement out of 'The Cornish Riviera' publication of 1905.

Chapter Nine

Tourism

The Regency period and the early years of Victorian England saw the development of much fine architecture in Penzance with fashionable terraces and squares bringing elegance and dignity to the town. In *Excursions through Cornwall* (1824) F.W. Stockdale spoke favourably:

'Penzance has long been noted for the pleasantness of its situation, the salubrity of its air and the beauty of its natives; it is in consequence much resorted by the invalids who, in most instances, have derived more benefit than they had anticipated. Indeed, the mildness of the climate of Penzance is often compared to that of Italy, and by a late writer is even said to surpass it. Owing to improvements made of late years, and the erection of several new buildings, Penzance has become a very populous and highly respectable Town, and altogether possesses as many claims to patronage as any watering place in the kingdom.'

Penzance promenade was constructed in 1844, making a great contribution to the image and the appeal of the town as a resort. As an attraction it was considered to be 'unequalled anywhere in the west', and became the focal point of the town for visitors.

Almost immediately after the establishment of through railway services, the Queens Hotel was built in a central position on the promenade itself. It opened from 1861 as the premier accommodation of the growing resort and was extended considerably in 1871 and again in 1908. *Murray's Handbook for Cornwall and Devon* (1859) emphasised the services of the railway to Penzance and recommended its readers to make excursions to places of local interest such as Logan Rock, Lamorna Cove and St. Michael's Mount. *The West Briton* acknowledged the railway in September 1861:

Penzance promenade looking westward towards Newlyn in 1935. Many of the important features for a popular holiday are seen here — the broad sea front itself, the 'Cafe Marine', the Beachfied Hotel, immediately opposite, and next to that, the Winter Gardens ballroom. The Pavillion Theatre is also prominent in the right foreground, and the line of coaches offering a variety of local excursions provides a definite holiday atmosphere.

M. Gendall

'The number of visitors to Penzance and its neighbourhood this season has been altogether unprecedented, ... and it is stated that since the opening of the Cornwall Railway, many pictures of scenes in Cornwall have been exhibited.'

The baths built on a central site along the promenade were also extended in view of the increased demand, and were well regarded for their position and their excellent views over Mount's Bay.

Local excursion traffic also became popular. An early and interesting example on the West Cornwall Railway dates from July 1855. This was the well publicised and popular Temperance outing from Truro to Penzance. It was reported that 1,016 people joined the train at Truro requiring forty-five coaches and motive power of no less than three locomotives. Large numbers also met the train at intermediate stations at Camborne so that on arrival at Penzance, the train consisted of eighty-four coaches. Because of the number of people involved that day the locomotives were required to return to Hayle and St. Ives Road (St. Erth) to pick up those passengers left waiting. This working alone amounted to twenty-six coaches. The normal timetabled train from Truro was also increased by ten coaches from Camborne to meet demand, and the press recorded that some 5,612 people visited Penzance by train that day with traffic receipts amounting to £285. 19s. 5d.

During the next season, in August 1856, there was another particularly eventful excursion organised by the Penzance Wesleyan Association. A train was chartered to Truro for an annual outing but in the event it became a definite catalogue of disasters. Apart from the very wet weather on this occasion, a Mr. Andrew Noall, one of the party from St. Ives, died of apoplexy en route; and on the return journey the train was subject to a derailment at St. Erth station. Having overcome this problem the train eventually terminated at the eastern end of the viaduct at Penzance on account of heavy seas and storm damage: the passengers ended their day by walking the remaining distance along the roadside.

Excursion traffic gradually became more wide-ranging and ambitious once the facilities for through rail travel were made possible. In June 1860, Thomas Cook organised an excursion from Scotland to Land's End. Details are sparse, but 400 people arrived at Truro in an eight coached train, 'of whom 300 went on to Penzance'.

The theme of growing popularity was often repeated in the newspapers during the 1860s and by the final year of that decade it was said: 'Penzance is now the resort of a great number of visitors from all parts of the kingdom'. Similarly, Marazion and St. Michael's Mount received numbers of visitors that:

'exceeded any corresponding month in the memory of any inhabitants. ... Every respectable lodging house has for some time been full and tourists frequently seek accommodation in vain.' (September 1869)

Excursion traffic was encouraged and combined rail and steamer trips opened out the area bringing a new perspective to travel. One such example was that of August 1871 when the Cornwall Railway organised an excursion by train from Plymouth early in the morning to Penzance, there to meet the paddle steamer Earl of Arran:

'waiting to convey excursionists along the south coast of Cornwall to view St. Michael's Mount, Mullion Island, Kynance Cove and the Lizard etc. .... as fares are so low many will doubtless sieze the opportunity of seeing Cornwall's beauties by sea and land.'

More ambitious projects included excursions from Penzance and Plymouth to Guernsey and Jersey, again as combined rail and sea workings.

Two very positive steps were taken in 1876 to promote business for the resort. At the cost of 60 guineas on the part of the town, two pages were taken in Thomas Cook's travel literature, and, significantly, Penzance published its first official guide to the resort. A guide book to Penzance had been published, as early as 1852. It included views and illustrations of the locality, a descriptive/historical narrative and a map. This publication was printed in Penzance by E. Rowe and Son, selling at 6/- each. Both these developments indicated the growing popularity of Penzance and the intention on the part of the town to enhance its image as a fashionable resort. By modern standards the *Guide* was an extremely modest, reserved production in keeping with the character of the period. Four important hotels were included and it is worth making a mention of them to illustrate the prevailing atmosphere. The Mounts Bay Hotel advertised 'Suites of apartments for Families of Distinction .. invalids will find the comforts of home'. The Union Hotel stressed its facilities for travel around the district. 'A Four Horse Brake leaves the hotel every day in the season (Sundays excepted) for the Land's End, Logan Rock and Sennen . . . . also an omnibus to the Lizard passes the Hotel daily.' The Queens Hotel was extended within ten years of its opening (1861) in order to meet demand and, like all the major establishments it provided transport to and from the station, making it a policy to meet every train arriving at Penzance. In terms of general information, the *Guide* detailed facilities such as local excursions, amateur fishing, botany and historical reference, and it stressed convincing features on temperatures, sunshine and rainfall. The overall impression of Penzance, given at this time, was of an expanding resort that showed clear evidence of the desire to provide for its visitors in the appropriate manner. On a visit to Logan Rock in 1870, however, the celebrated Parson Kilvert registered his disapproval of some would-be tourists. With a note of definite derision, he described one particular party as: ' A rude vulgar crew of tourists grinning like dogs'.

The visit of the Prince and Princess of Wales on 24th July 1865 was an important occasion for the town and a source of valuable excursion traffic for the railway. Penzance was one of a number of locations visited by the Royal Yacht, *Osborne*, each attracting large numbers of people. The Royal Party visited Land's End and St. Michael's Mount, and also descended Botallack Mine, near St. Just. Alexandra Road was officially named and opened by the Princess, and during the evening there were appropriate celebrations, including: 'One of the most brilliant firework demonstrations which has ever been known in the West of England'. Bonfires were lit along the coastline, and on the hills and tar barrells were burned on the Promenade, and along the harbour walls. The large crowds gathered at the Promenade were also treated to the spectacle of an old schooner set alight offshore, to burn 'gloriously for several hours'.

In its report on the event, *The West Briton* noted:

'The Royal Visit has been the cause of a harvest to the railway companies. On Monday morning the West Cornwall Railway brought over 5,000 people to Penzance. . . . .'

Five years later on 5th March 1870 the Queen of the Netherlands also made a very brief visit to Land's End. The party arrived by the morning Mail train to be met by the mayor and Town Council. Lunch was provided at the Queens Hotel and the Queen left the town by train during the afternoon for Torquay. Large numbers of people were again drawn to Penzance for the occasion.

Numerous public entertainments and occasions also generated useful excursion traffic. Amongst the more noteable were: 'The Mounts Bay and West of England Races', Mounts Bay Regatta and the Annual Swimming Gala, all held at

Penzance, the latter drawing 2,500 people to the town in August 1871. Events such as the National Wesleyan Conference, also brought special trains from Paddington to Penzance in 1888.

From the beginning of the season in 1875 Thomas Cook and Co. came into active participation in Cornish excursion traffic, thereby, widening the scope for tourism by providing opportunities for increased business from people of more modest means. An itinerary was issued for a new series of tours to include all the principle places of interest from Bristol to the Land's End. Special arrangements were made with the railways, steamboat, coach and hotel proprietors, with 'very moderate' fares. Arrangements were made for a total of 32 tours overall. *The West Briton* reported on arrangements for a tour in 1877:

'Mr. Cook, well known excursionist manager, has published a list of fifteen Cornish Hotels which accept Cook's Hotel Company at a uniform rate of 11/- per day. This includes meat breakfast 2/6d; dinner of four courses 3/-; plain tea 1/6d; bed 2/6d; and attendances 1/6d. What would our forefathers say of a trip from London to Truro, Hayle, Penzance, Isles of Scilly, Helston, the Lizard, Kynance Cove, Falmouth and back to London – all for £2 3s.?'

By 1878 there was further positive news to relate in regard to tourism: Penzance station was to be rebuilt on a larger and more imposing scale, to reflect growing prosperity and confidence. In September 1880, for example, *The West Briton* recorded: 'Penzance continues to be very full of visitors and some of the hotels have needed to find beds 'out'. Upwards of 200 persons a week are crossing to the Isles of Scilly.'

Before the end of the century, Penzance had provided two definitively Victorian attractions for its visitors and residents: new Public Baths at the western end of the Promenade in 1887, and the famous Morrab Gardens opened in 1889. *Black's Guide* gave details of the Baths: 'These are Public Baths with a seawater swimming basin, beside which a small Pavillion has been built for entertainment, and bathing machines beyond.' No Victorian or Edwardian resort would have been complete without its bathing machines and the etiquette of the Baths was definitive of the period. Facilities were reserved each day from 10.00 a.m. until noon for the use of the ladies only. Morrab Park also deserved its excellent reputation. With its elegant lawns, ornamental fountains and ponds, its rare sub-tropical plants and trees, and its inevitable bandstand (1897), the park characterised the resort in a dignified and unique setting. *The Great Western Railway Guide to Penzance* in 1908 conveyed the atmosphere magnificently:

'If the pilgrim to Penzance walks in Morrab Gardens where a good band plays amongst a wealth of sub-tropical vegetation which Nice or Monte Carlo might envy, he may without any stretch of the imagination fancy himself in Algeria.'

Favourable comparisons with the continent were numerous as Penzance increased in popularity. *Kelly's Directory* of 1883 considered the climate 'equal to that of Madeira or the South of France . . . . admirably adapted to invalids as a winter resort'. In 1900 *The Tourist's Guide to Cornwall and the Isles of Scilly* maintained: 'For situation Penzance has been frequently compared with the Riviera and at present lacks only continental popularity'. *Black's Guide* also reported that:

'No other resort has laid itself out for winter patients as well as Penzance, especially in the way of outdoor and indoor recreations and good accommodation.'

Such comparisons were to reach their height in the later work of S.P. Mais, who stated, unequivocally, in *The Cornish Riviera* of 1928: 'Penzance is proving to be a formidable rival to Madeira. the Scillies to the Azores and Mullion to Monte Carlo.'

Great Western publicity was always alert to the task of positive comparison with the fashionable venues of Europe,

Black's Guide described Mounts Bay in likeness to 'the brilliant hues of the Mediterranean', and, *The Tourists' Guide to Cornwall* emphasised the setting as, 'a series of attractions hard to rival'. The GWR also prepared a series of striking visual parallels drawing on all the imagery of a Riviera climate. One particularly effective example was a poster of 1908 that successfully drew similarities between Cornwall and Italy in terms of geographical setting, physical resemblance, climate and cultural heritage. Headed: *See Your Own Country First*, it was a clever and an inspired work of promotion. In the same vein, St. Michael's Mount was set alongside Mont St. Michel in Brittany. There was real pride in the association with St. Michael's Mount as an outstanding attraction and the Great Western featured it on many occasions in their poster work. The company's first promotional publication was appropriately, *The Cornish Riviera* in 1904, conveying the imagery and ideal of a unique setting in Britain. *The English Riviera* by J.H. Stone also described Penzance as, 'a mixture of Bath, Cheltenham and Torquay rolled into one'.

The Edwardian years brought considerable activity and achievement at Penzance. It was during this time that the Queen's Hotel was again enlarged and many significant new attractions were developed. A particular feature during this period was the provision of public gardens along the sea front area. In 1903 the small but neat Alexandra Gardens were opened on the Promenade, and in 1914 a much larger project was developed at the western end of the Promenade: the Bolitho Gardens. This was an ambitious scheme involving landscaping effects, shrubberies, lawns and palm trees, thereby emphasising the character of a Cornish Riviera, indeed it was frequently used in Great Western publicity on account of its luxurian associations at the water's edge. A further development of 1916, during the Great War, was the construction of an ornamental gardens immediately west of the Promenade. This was also the initiative of the Bolitho family and was referred to variously as the Wherrytown Gardens, the Bolitho Sunken Gardens or the 'Italianate Gardens', 'daringly constructed on the verge of the sea – much frequented by delicate people'.

In 1905 a bandstand was built on the Promenade itself, opposite the Queen's Hotel, where the Town Band gave concerts each weekday evening during the season from 7.30 p.m. to 9.30 p.m. The Pavillion Theatre, also situated on the Promenade, was opened in 1911, incorporating a roof garden and cafe; whilst the following year saw the opening of the first cinema in the town. A GWR bus service also gave access to the golf links west of the town at a return fare of one shilling. Green fees for visitors were listed: Gents, two shillings a day, 7/6 per week or £1 per month. Corresponding fees for ladies were set at two shillings, five shillings and fifteen shillings.

Great Western omnibuses also began services to many of the surrounding districts together with several locally owned concerns. Lands End, Cape Cornwall and St. Just, Marazion, Porthleven and the entire Lizard peninsula were all well within reach and local boat owners organised trips to many places along the shore of Mounts Bay, working from the harbour and the landing stages at the promenade. There were also of course the attractions of the Isles of Scilly reached by steamer from Penzance.

The *GWR Guide to Cornwall for 1908* gave the fares for holiday travel from Paddington. A first class fare to Penzance was 75/-; second class was 50/-; and third class 40/-. The high costs involved limited travel to those who could afford such prices, and for many working people special excursions provided the only means to enjoy a journey over any distance. On 23 May 1907, for example, 1,178 cotton spinners and weavers from Manchester visited Penzance for a day. Tickets were issued at 12s. 6d. each and the train departed from Manchester at 10.30

p.m. arriving at Penzance at 10.50 a.m. on the Friday morning. The excursion returned late the same day.

An excellent opportunity for excursion traffic to Penzance came in July 1910 when King George V and Queen Mary visited Mounts Bay for the Royal Review of the Fleet. The mayor of Penzance lost no time in writing to the divisional superintendant of the GWR pointing out the important role of the railway, but the Company needed little encouragement and was eager to participate in this prestigious occasion. Excursion fares were granted on both a local and long distance basis. Arrangements were made for cheap tickets to be available to Penzance from Thursday 21 July, and during the following weekdays for as long as the Fleet remained in Mounts Bay. Special 'day' excursions were also offered from Paddington.

In concluding the details on the period prior to World War One, it is interesting to note the views of one correspondent of the local newspaper. Writing on tourism, by 1914 he observed:

'Cornish fishing villages have changed a great deal since visiting there twenty years ago. Amongst the factors involved is the ever increasing influx of well-to-do visitors – the cost of long railway journeys from London and the provincial cities squeezes out the cheaper trippers which is rapidly transforming some of the Cornish fishing ports into holiday resorts. An advance in cost of living is bound to follow sooner or later; at present there are two sets of prices, one for the visitors, the other for locals. Experiences teach that the quest for 'a good let' kills fishing – all along the south coast small colonies of fishing have disappeared as the result of the development of seaside villages into popular holiday resorts.'

The commercial success and promotional achievements of the 'Holiday Line' during the period between the Wars owed a great deal to the particular managerial qualities of Felix Pole. His appointment as General Manager in 1921 marked the development of a detailed programme of work seeking to promote Great Western holiday resorts through the activities of the publicity department, established in 1924, and the direct participation of the resorts themselves. Pole envisaged ambitious co-ordinated schemes wherein the company and the resorts worked together to maximise their efforts; his aim being to express the ideal of undisputed excellence, both in the quality of the environment and the pursuit of dedicated professional services. The company's literary works such as *The Ocean Coast*, 1925, and the new edition of *The Cornish Riviera*, 1928, gave expression to the unique character of Great Western resorts, but the management was also concerned to ensure that facilities at, and between, the resorts fulfilled their particular requirements. To achieve the high standards of service, the company eventually introduced generous schemes of assistance for those resorts willing to participate in positive publicity, thereby, interpreting the slogan 'Go Great Western', in its widest sense. In tourism, the company could only be as good as the resorts it served; and the resorts, only as good as the service they received from the railway. Pole's achievement was to both formulate this and give it actual expression in positive commercial practice.

The formation of the 'Come to Cornwall' Association in 1929 served to focus timely attention on questions of promotion and policy in tourism within the county. Penzance Chamber of Commerce and the GWR took an active interest in this development not only for its immediate effect on the resort, but for the longer term issues that it served to emphasise, particularly questions as to the future character and status of Penzance as a resort.

In itself the 'Come to Cornwall' Association was a collective concern on the part of the leading resorts to promote the county as a whole. It was anticipated that with their positive co-operation, the resorts within the scheme, would all be linked to one central bureau for purposes of publicity and information. The intention was, obviously, to provide the best possible arrangements for tourists to enjoy all that Cornwall might have to offer. This was stated at the time, as the desire, 'to link up the whole of Cornwall through one bureau so that a visitor could pass from one town to another and feel that all his wants were attended to'. It was good news for the GWR who welcomed this initiative in the county, but Sir Felix Pole stressed that, as an important initiative, it had come twenty years too late. He pointed to current examples of this successful practice in Europe where resorts were seen to work together without a climate of rivalry and jealousy dividing them. Cooperation, he argued, 'will be amply rewarded by the increased volume of business'.

There was particular significance in Pole's expressed regret that this new policy was long overdue and there is reason to believe that by this time the GWR was becoming anxious about certain aspects of the tourist business at Penzance. With the decline of former industries such as tin, and in some respects, fishing, many people saw tourism as the means to future prosperity. At the same time, the Great Western, along with particular local support, was attempting to persuade the town council and the chamber of commerce to invest in the resort. It was imperative, they argued, to put money and resources into extended advertising and into new amenities, if the resort was to develop and continue to attract tourists in increasing numbers. Bournemouth was mentioned by way of example in discussion on finance development; and in this case it was pointed out that that resort had in recent times spent over a quarter of a million pounds on entertainment facilities. Nearer to home, Newquay had taken full advantage of its growing popularity, and GWR pressure for investment and growth led the local community at Penzance to an assessment and evaluation of its position as a tourist centre. It was, therefore, a time of decision; and it became clear that during the 1930s the town, if sometimes reluctantly, had to reach beyond the circumstances and character of a latter-day watering place, and give careful thought to its position, commercially. Penzance, unlike Newquay, of course, still had an identity as a trading port, and this was also an important consideration in determining the future pattern of development.

Another of Felix Pole's observations, on matters of accommodation, is also instructive for present purposes. He was aware that many Cornish boarding houses and hotels were being enlarged and improved, but thought it 'a pity that many could not be blown up and entirely rebuilt!' His remarks lead us on to consider the resort in the wider context of accommodation and public health generally.

Since the early days of the railway at Penzance there was a close correlation between railway influences, tourism and an overall improvement in public health. In 1888, for example, the town clerk, on behalf of the council, and the Sanitary Authority, wrote to certain significant resorts for copies of their bye-laws. Those consulted were: Torquay, Plymouth, Bournemouth, Teignmouth, Hastings, Margate and Southport. By the third decade of the twentieth century high standards were imperative. The mayor emphasised this to the Chamber of Commerce:

'Penzance prides itself as a health resort and must essentially be capable of providing a good water supply and a clean bill of health as far as drainage is concerned, and I suggest that it will be a major boon to the place.'

It was more a prerequisite than a boon for tourism, even if one could deal with tourism in isolation! The mayor's statement from January 1930 was part of an important announcement dealing with a projected £24,000 scheme. In 1878 the Great Western had, in fact, laid the main sewer leading to the outfall in the station area of the town and once again, in 1930, they offered the services

Just west of Angarrack Viaduct and milepost 318, No. 4086 *Builth Castle* climbs the bank towards Gwinear Road with a heavy Penzance — Sheffield working on 4th July 1959. Note the original alignment of the West Cornwall Railway to the right of the train. Once across Angarrack Viaduct the gradient stiffens to give, at its worst, one mile at 1 in 61. The whole section from Hayle to Gwinear Road was heavily engineered, winding and climbing all the way.

P.Q. Treloar

of the chief engineer to work in conjunction with the borough surveyor and give assistance accordingly. The holiday guides and publicity for the resort, generally, stressed the installation of 'full modern conveniences' or 'latest sanitary arrangements', particularly amongst the more expensively priced accommodation and it does reflect an important consideration of the time. That it needed to be emphasised at all, is a measure of the differences that separate us today from an age, relatively speaking, not that far removed from our own. It is sufficient to note now that these fundamental concerns such as water supply and sanitation were being taken very seriously by both the resort and the GWR not least for their bearing on tourism.

Sir Felix Pole had expressed his views in general terms on matters of tourist accommodation in Cornwall with his regrets that it was often less than satisfactory. The company's attitude was clear. They would do all they could to attract visitors to the town, but it was then the duty of the town to provide, once their tourists had actually arrived. This would suggest that there could well have been difficulties and disputes over the provision of accommodation, however discreet the exchanges outwardly. The provision for instance, of extra mid-week excursion fares (Tuesday and Wednesday) during the summer season of 1929 from Paddington at the normal weekend excursion ticket rate encouraged large numbers of people to take advantage of the opportunity to visit West Cornwall. This, however, caused problems at Penzance in catering for them, with the local press reporting that '. . . difficulties were being experienced in finding sufficient accommodation on arrival'. In the same year, the local council sounded the company on the possibilities of a new hotel for the resort along the lines of Tregenna Castle at St. Ives, which was to be modernised and extended. The company certainly increased its involvement with the town during the 1930s, but a new hotel, as a direct company initiative, did not materialise.

An interesting innovation by the Great Western in 1934, however, was the camping coach. These provided useful, if limited, facilities and they reflected something of the vogue for camping and related activities, popular at this time. A camping coach was sited at Marazion, in the south sidings, behind the station and overlooking Mounts Bay. It was advertised in the pages of *Holiday Haunts* and for the season of 1938, the charges at Marazion were £4 per week, for the class C eight berth accommodation. A minimum of six rail tickets were required in order to secure the coach. Another was provided at Lelant, also a class C rating. Elsewhere in Cornwall at that time camping coaches were provided at Fowey, Luxulyan, Perranwell, and St. Agnes. In the post war years these facilities were also extended to St. Erth and St. Ives in the immediate West Cornwall area.

Typical third class monthly returns from major areas in 1938, for example, were: Paddington 53/3d; Manchester 66/3d; Sheffield 65/1d; Birmingham 52/-; and Swansea 52/6d. Holiday season tickets from Penzance covering the area eastward to Truro, Newquay and Falmouth were also available. Prices for one week's travel were: First Class 15/9d, and Second Class 10/6d.

Penzance, Land's End and St. Ives also featured in a 'Land Cruise' on the 'Cornish Riviera' for six days in the summer season from mid May to mid September. The six day tour from Paddington was priced at £13, including First Class rail accommodation and hotel facilities. A GWR representative accompanied each tour.

From Paddington, passengers travelled by train to Torquay. From there motor coaches were employed in order to visit Buckfast Abbey, Dartmoor, Tavistock, Launceston, Tintagel, Newquay, Perranporth, Penzance, Lands End, St. Ives, Falmouth, Truro, Plymouth and Torquay. The return journey to

London was then made by train. Whilst this type of tour was only partly linked with Penzance and St. Ives it did, however, act as a valuable promotional development for the area, as the early tours of Thomas Cook had done in the 1870s.

The proceedings at the annual Penzance Chamber of Commerce banquet in January 1936 were also particularly instructive in regard to the position on tourism at the resort. Mr. F.R. Potter, Superintendant of the GWR and Major Dewar, Publicity Officer, attended on behalf of the Company and spoke at length on their perspective and proposals.

In their remarks to the assembly, the superintendant and the publicity officer both emphasised the necessity for increased publicity, for improved arrangements on entertainments and accommodation, and for an extended season, beginning earlier in the year. Their theme was, primarily, one of the need for progress and change.

On publicity, it was disclosed that the company was prepared to subsidise the resort for the coming season to the extent that they would provide fifteen shillings for every £1 spent by the council on promoting the town and the surrounding district. This was not an entirely new scheme, as the GWR had already introduced the subsidy principle for earlier seasons with favourable response, where it was implemented positively. As an example for 1936, Newquay voted to spend £600 on advertising and the company, in turn, contributed a further £500. In that same year, however, Penzance chose to spend only £200. At that time, Major Dewar had emphasised that the prosperity of Cornwall was the prosperity of Newquay and any other holiday resort that realised the value of the cooperative scheme. For 1938 however, it was also made clear, in a firm, but polite manner, that the town should provide its own scheme to publicise the resort and that money would need to be spent.

With regard to entertainment and accommodation, Mr. Potter was forthright:

'There is no place I know of in the country which is more amenable to a winter resort than Penzance, but what you lack at the moment is entertainment to attract our visitors. We want to see also that your hotels and accommodation are adequate for our visitors.'

It was stressed, however, that the GWR had considerable regard for Penzance which was apparent in the considerable current investment of some £134,000 on new station facilities. Major Dewar also stressed the theme of change. He spoke on the need for an extension of the season as a means of improving both the spread and the volume of trade, whilst helping with the pressure on accommodation in peak months. It was hoped that more visitors might be attracted during May, June or September, but it was, once again, emphasised that primarily it was the railway's task to bring the tourist to the resort; it was the responsibility of the town to provide once they had arrived.

In response, the members of the chamber of commerce let it be known that they had considerable affection for the GWR. This was expressed in an open manner: 'One of the best friends Penzance has got is the Great Western Railway; ... they have always been most generous to us'. It was also pointed out by the local chairman, however, that Penzance was, a 'seaport town and not merely a seaside resort'. This was significant particularly when it came to comparisons, favourable or otherwise, with resorts elsewhere. It was also a factor certain to influence decisions on the future character and identity of the town.

One further significant development no-one could afford to overlook, however, was the introduction of the Holidays with Pay Act, passed by Parliament that same year. The provision for annual paid holidays entitled a further 11 million people to one week's leave from work, and was a great incentive for tourist traffic. It must also have been a major consideration on the part of the GWR in their overall proposals for Penzance.

The introduction of paid holidays reflected the climate of change in tourism generally. There was evidence of a shifting pattern with the industry, looking to a new style and format, possibly best expressed in the opening of the first holiday camp at Skegness in 1937, and echoed at Penzance in the call for increased leisure amenities. The traditionally reserved and circumscribed nature of tourism was, therefore, in the process of gradual, but clearly perceptible, change; a more robust industry, with a much broader commercial basis, began to emerge.

Penzance had, during the thirties, introduced several important projects in the interests of tourism. In particular, the eastern end of the promenade had been entirely re-developed, involving the demolition of what had been a very poor housing area adjoining the harbour. Earlier again, in 1923 a new road access was developed to improve links between the harbour area and the promenade, but in 1933 and 1935 the major work was carried out.

At Whitsun 1933 the town council opened St. Anthony Gardens, on the site of the former housing complex. It was landscaped development that incorporated fountains, terraced seating, shrubberies and grassed areas overlooking Mounts Bay. Two years later the Jubilee Bathing Pool was opened on a site immediately opposite the gardens. Floodlights and a spacious layout made it an attractive proposition.

The new bathing pool was clearly representative of the new style of facility at the town and the Great Western were quick to feature it in their publicity on the resort. Three years after it opened this substantial new development was further improved at a cost of £650; Sunday opening was also introduced, but only under protest. The entire seafront from Newlyn in the west to Penzance harbour, in the east, now consisted of promenade, garden and bathing pool facilities, reflecting a very positive image for tourists. Moreover, increased amenities such as tennis courts, bowling and putting greens along the seafront were also indicative of more active pursuits to cater for holiday interests. A lavishly equipped modern cinema was also opened in 1935 at the same time as many chain stores begain to appear in the main shopping streets. Publicity itself was more vigorous and robust during the 1930s. The traditional imagery of the Cornish Riviera was still conveyed, but there was careful emphasis upon the newer style facilities to attract a wider cross-section of holiday makers.

By way of final reference to tourist development within the resort, it is important to note the increased activity of road transport. In particular, the provision of three municipal car parks, 'with uniformed attendants', and the presence of at least three coach tour operators could scarcely be ignored. Competition for traffic from road transport was a major development and in the long-term would prove to be a decisive factor in influencing and shaping the character of the district, just as the railway had done in the previous century. In railway terms, however, this period marked the last important initiative of the GWR, whereby the company, ironically, provided the basis for the successful handling of extensive holiday traffic under British Railways from 1948.

When war broke out in 1939, it did not bring an entire era to a close: it hastened the process of change which was already apparent. The basic pattern for the more immediate post-war years was established during the 1930s; the only major difference being in number, with increased opportunity for wider interests. In overall character and ethos, for example, tourism in the early fifties at Penzance was not far removed from the late thirties. With the growth of more affluent times from the closing years of the 1950s, however, conditions were to alter considerably.

Chapter Ten

The Isles of Scilly, Light Railway Projects, GWR Bus Services

In his 1935 publication *The Isle of the Island*, S.P. Mais said of the Scilly Isles: 'They come very close to my idea of the Garden of Eden'. They are, indeed, unique to Britain in regard to their setting, character and climate; the flower industry is well known and the islands attract large numbers of tourists. In their situation, 26 miles west of Lands End, the Islands offer something different from mainland life, and at the same time they are no longer particularly remote.

Close links with the mainland date from 1858 when The Scilly Isles Steam Navigation Company began a regular service from Penzance with the steamer *Little Western*. Prior to this the islands were extremely isolated. In March 1871 the Company amalgamated with the West Cornwall Railway and a new ven-

year, 250 baskets of flowers were sent to Penzance, comprising, 'the largest consignment ever sent'. The first recorded consignment, baskets of lilies, dated from March 1874. Flower traffic grew rapidly. In 1886, 85 tons were sent to the mainland, whilst the figures for 1896, 1924 and 1931 were: 514 tons; 709 tons and 1,064 tons respectively.

Tourism became very popular with improved access. *Kelly's Directory* for 1914 included the details of steamer services. 'A steamer leaves twice a week in winter and three times in summer, except in May and June when there are daily services'. The *GWR Guide of 1908* offered advice for travellers anxious to reach the Islands quickly:

Packing the flowers for shipment to the mainland and the railway. This late nineteenth century view of the interior of a cottage on the Isles of Scilly shows how the entire family would be involved in the work. It gives us an excellent insight into the life style of the islanders and was taken by an expert photographer of the day.
Cornwall County Museum

ture was formed: The West Cornwall Steamship Company, based at Penzance. Services were increased with the introduction of another ship, *The Earl of Arran*, a 144 ton iron paddle steamer.

The new company provided good opportunities to develop fish and vegetable traffic from the Islands, and regular sailings in conjunction with rail services also strengthened ties with the mainland. Tourism and the flower industry followed soon after. By 1883 prospective visitors could purchase *Tonkins Guide to the Scilly Islands*, published locally at Penzance. Early that same

'If you are in a hurry, leave Paddington at 9 p.m. enjoy a comfortable night's rest in the sleeping car and wake up in time to catch a passing glance of *Majestic Michael*. Breakfast at your leisure in Penzance in a sunny room overlooking Mounts Bay; go on board at 10, and lunch luxuriantly on the *SS Lyonesse*.'

Advertisements for two of the Islands' hotels, Tregarthen and Holgates, carried full page status in the GWR Guide, highlighting 'Hot and cold fresh and salt water baths, ladies drawing rooms, modern sanitation', and 'the attractions of fishing, boating, bathing, golf and tennis'. The GWR relished its close identity with such a unique part of the country and made a special point of promoting the Islands as a unique location in Britain.

Whilst the Isles of Scilly enjoyed growth and prosperity, particularly by the turn of the century, the mainland communities west of Penzance were anxious to see the railway extended to serve their area directly.

In April and May 1898 two applications were made for Orders under the Light Railway Acts. During April the Penzance, Newlyn and St. Just Light Railway Company applied for an Order, followed by The Lands End and Great Western Joint; two separate undertakings.

The former planned to link Penzance and Newlyn harbour by means of an electric railway running along the quayside and across the promenade to Newlyn. A steam worked section was considered too disruptive given the hotels and tourist attractions en route. From Newlyn the line would run north-west through Newlyn Coombe towards Buryas Bridge, thence past Sancreed to St. Just. The Lands End and Great Western Joint planned for a junction with the Great Western main line east of Marazion station from where the line ran westward serving Heamoor,

Sancreed, St. Buryan and Sennen. The potential for vegetable traffic, china clay, (from two sites), coal and dairy produce together with general goods was stressed, and on 11 August 1898 the Commissioners considered the applications under the Light Railway Inquiry.

The Commissioners were 'strongly impressed with the need for better railway facilities in the district', but reluctantly they were forced to reject both schemes. They did not consider the mileage sufficient to justify two separate administrations, and they were critical of the fact that no provision was made for a junction at Sancreed. The latter was considered by the Commissioners to be the obvious site for a central junction. It was also stressed that the proposals did not serve the best interests of the community overall, and the rejection would, therefore, give the opportunity for 'a revised and more mature scheme'.

A further Order followed on 22 November 1898. The junction with the main line to Penzance was to be sited 450 yards east of Marazion level crossing and from that point the line ran westward past Gulval, Heamoor and Tremethick Cross to a junction at Sancreed, east of the village. From Sancreed, lines were prospected to St. Just, Lands End and Newlyn.

Proposed Light Railways West of Penzance—1898

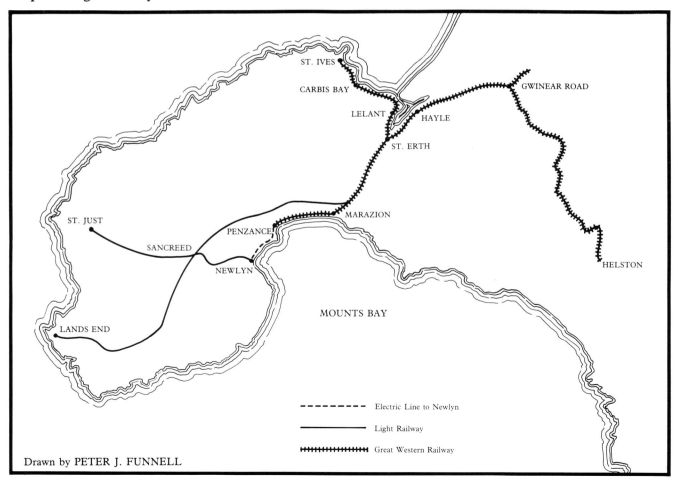

Drawn by PETER J. FUNNELL

- - - - - - - - Electric Line to Newlyn

———————— Light Railway

++++++++++++++++ Great Western Railway

The route to St. Just followed in a westerly direction across the moorland to approach the town from the south-east. The terminus was to be built at the southern end of Fore Street. Plans for the line to Newlyn followed a similar route to that described earlier, terminating at the landward end of the North Pier. A third line to Lands End reflected the concern shown earlier for an adequate service for St. Buryan and St. Levan. It ran in a south-westerly direction from Sancreed to St. Buryan and Crean, then turned west to pass Poljigga, Trevescan and Sennen to terminate at a point, '150 yards east of the front door of Lands End Hotel'. Two short branches to china clay works were also planned as part of the overall scheme.

These proposals promised a new perspective for railways in West Cornwall, but despite their potential value to the community, openly acknowledged by the Commissioners, the lines were never built. Like the similar scheme to build a Light Railway from Helston to the Lizard, in 1897, they offer a fascinating insight into that which might have been, but for changing circumstances.

One reason why the railway was not extended beyond Penzance was the introduction of a number of bus services operated by the Great Western. The buses provided an acceptable alternative and first ran from Helston to the Lizard on 17 August 1903. They were soon operating at Penzance; the first service to Marazion beginning on 31 October 1903. In the following year buses began working to Lands End and St. Just, on 3 April and the 16 May respectively. Services were gradually extended to cover the district, contributing directly to the improvement of communication and trade, and to the status of the GWR in the community.

ROAD MOTOR-CAR SERVICES.

Between
PENZANCE STATION, MARAZION STATION, AND MARAZION.

MOTOR OMNIBUSES.—WEEK DAYS ONLY

LEAVE PENZANCE STATION FOR MARAZION AT	LEAVE MARAZION STATION FOR MARAZION AT	LEAVE MARAZION FOR MARAZION AND PENZANCE STATIONS AT
a.m.	a.m.	a.m.
7 45	7 55	8 15
9 30	9 40	10 0
		noon.
11 30	11 40	12 0
p.m.	p.m.	p.m.
1 30	1 40	2 0
3 0	3 10	3 30
4 0	4 10	4 30
5 0	5 10	5 30
6 0	6 10	6 30
7 0	7 10	7 30
8 0	8 10	8 30
T9 30	T9 40	T10 0

T—Thursdays and Saturdays only.

FARES.

Penzance Station and Marazion Station	3d.	Penzance Station and Marazion Town	3d.
Marazion Station and Marazion Town	1d.	„ „ Long Rock	2d.

Between HELSTON AND THE LIZARD.

TO THE LIZARD.

		WEEK DAYS ONLY.	
		a.m.	a.m.
		7 45	11 45
HELSTON (Station) ... ... dep.			
DODSON'S GAP (for G'nwallo') „			
CURY CROSS LANES (for Cury) „		CALLING AT THESE PLACES IF REQUIRED.	
PENHALE (for Mullion) „			
RUAN CROSS ROADS (for Cadgwith) „			
HOUSEL ROAD ... ... „			
THE LIZARD ... ... arr.		9 0	12 55

FROM THE LIZARD.

		WEEK DAYS ONLY.	
		a.m.	p.m.
		9 15	4 15
THE LIZARD ... ... dep.			
HOUSEL ROAD ... ... „			
RUAN CROSS ROAD (for Cadgwith) „			
PENHALE (for Mullion) „		CALLING AT THESE PLACES IF REQUIRED.	
CURY CROSS LANES (for Cury) „			
DODSON'S GAP (for G'nwallo') „			
HELSTON (Station) ... ... arr.		10 25	5 30

ROAD MOTOR-CAR SERVICES—continued.
Between HELSTON AND THE LIZARD—continued.

FARES.

Between	Helston.	Dodson's Gap.	Cury Cross Lanes.	Penhale.	Ruan Cross Roads.
	s. d.	s. d.	s. d.	s. d.	s. d.
DODSON'S GAP ...	0 6	...	...	...	...
CURY CROSS LANES ...	0 9	0 6	...	...	...
PENHALE (for Mullion) ...	1 0	0 9	0 6	...	...
RUAN CROSS ROADS ...	1 3	1 0	0 9	0 6	...
THE LIZARD ...	1 6	1 3	1 0	0 9	0 6

BOOKING SEATS.—Passengers may BOOK SEATS on the Motor Omnibuses at the Railway Stations, and at the Company's Receiving Office at The Lizard (Hill's) Hotel, for the THROUGH journey between Helston and The Lizard.

PENZANCE STATION AND ST. JUST.

To ST. JUST.		WEEK DAYS.					SUNDAYS
PENZANCE STATION ... dep.		a.m. 10 0	noon T12 0	p.m. 3 0	p.m. 6 0	p.m. 8 0	a.m. 10 45
GUILDHALL ... ... „							
TOP OF ALEX. ROAD ... „		CALLING AT THESE PLACES IF REQUIRED. Passengers may join the Omnibuses at any point between Guildhall and St. Just on payment of Fares from previous stage.					
TREMETHICK CROSS ... „							
NEW BRIDGE ... „							
PENDEEN ROAD ... „							
ST. JUST ... ... arr.		10 55	T12 55	3 55	6 55	8 55	11 40

FROM ST. JUST.		WEEK DAYS.					SUNDAYS
ST. JUST ... ... dep.		a.m. 9 0	a.m. T11 0	p.m. 2 0	p.m. 5 0	p.m 7 0	p.m. 4 0
PENDEEN ROAD ... „							
NEW BRIDGE ... „		CALLING AT THESE PLACES IF REQUIRED. Passengers may join the Omnibuses at any point between St. Just and Guildhall on payment of Fares from previous stage.					
TREMETHICK CROSS ... „							
TOP OF ALEX. ROAD ... „							
GUILDHALL ... ... „							
PENZANCE STATION ... arr.		9 50	T11 50	2 50	5 50	7 50	4 50

T—Thursdays and Saturdays only.

FARES.

Between	Penzance Station or Guildhall.	Tremethick Cross.	New Bridge.	Pendeen Road.
	s. d.	s. d.	s. d.	s. d.
TREMETHICK CROSS ...	0 3	...	...	...
NEW BRIDGE	0 4	0 3	...	...
PENDEEN ROAD	0 6	0 6	0 3	...
ST. JUST	0 9	0 9	0 6	0 3

Chapter Eleven

Post War Development

When nationalisation took effect in January 1948 there was little to indicate detailed change in appearance or working arrangements in West Cornwall. The GWR with its inbuilt resistance to change opposed the whole idea of nationalisation, and train services began gradually to shake off the effects of wartime and attempt a return to pre-war schedules, despite the climate of austerity.

There were some indications of new circumstances. Standard class Britannia Pacifics, for example, were drafted to work *The Cornish Riviera Express* during 1951, but theirs was a relatively short stay, limited to the early years of the decade. Nos. 70019 *Lightning* and 70024 *Vulcan* were two regular performers on this train. Standard design British Railways coaching stock was also introduced shortly afterwards on *The Cornish Riviera*, but even this appeared in the old GWR chocolate and cream livery from June 1956. Two other named expressed followed *The Cornishman* and *The Royal Duchy*, also turned out with full chocolate and cream sets. Outwardly, the railway system appeared as permanent as ever, as post-war traffic levels moved steadily to their peak.

Rail services to and from West Cornwall in 1959 were typical of the heavy traffic carried on both long distance and local workings during summer. The Saturday service together with details of local working is given here, reflecting a concentrated pattern, particularly at the local level. 1959 was also significant in as far as it marked the last year of intensive steam haulage in Cornwall, given the plan to eliminate steam in the West Country as soon as was practical.

The Modernisation Plan of 1955 had led to one important innovation in West Cornwall before the close of the decade. In April 1958 the diesel hydraulic D600 *Active*, first worked to Penzance. Thereafter, except for breakdown, these early Warship class locomotives began regular service on *The Cornish Riviera* with the locomotive from the 'down' train working back each evening at 7.00 p.m. on the Royal Mail. These 117 ton 8 cwt heavyweights were not a great success and were soon superceded by the lighter and more popular Swindon and North British design Warship class at only 78 tons. Withdrawals of steam locomotives followed rapidly, especially with the introduction of a further North British Type 2 design – the 6300 class. These were rated 1,100 B.H.P. other than the very earliest members of the class and they usually worked in pairs on trains such as *The Cornishman* or *Royal Duchy*. These smaller diesels also began work on the branch lines and on local freight turns, where again steam power was replaced. The Western class hydraulics at 2,700 B.H.P. were introduced at the end of 1961 by which time steam had largely disappeared from main line working.

Early and complete dieselisation throughout the West of England was the objective of Western Region management and was a scheme consistent with earlier proposals by the Great Western such as that in 1938 to electrify west of Taunton, or the oil firing experiments on main line working to Penzance in 1946/47. In each case it was recognised that savings could be made by eliminating long hauls to far west depots with locomotive coal: likewise expensive double-heading on the banks could be avoided. The West country was also ideal because it was a compact geographical unit, making it easy to administer.

No. 7018 *Drysllwyn Castle*, as fitted with a double chimney, approaches Long Rock crossing with a 'down' Manchester train on 28th November 1959. The locomotive is passing the site where today the line changes from double to single line for the remainder of the journey to the terminus. Beyond the 'up' line is the long siding reaching westward from Marazion yard. Telegraph poles and semaphore signals are no more than memories now, and the old assortment of stock shown here is in complete contrast with the standardised sets used today.   *M. Mensing*

Summer Saturday arrivals at Penzance in 1959:

Arrive		Depart	
5.50	Newcastle	3.40 p.m.	
6.05	Paddington	10.12 p.m.	
6.25	Paddington	10.35 p.m.	Sleeper
7.30	Paddington	9.50 p.m.	Sleeper via Bristol
8.25	Wolverhampton	9.50 p.m.	
8.40	Paddington	12.35 a.m.	Sleeper
9.05	Paddington	11.35 p.m.	Via Bristol
11.10	Paddington	11.50 p.m.	
11.30	Manchester	11.10 p.m.	
1.55	Liverpool	11.05 p.m.	
2.40	Paddington	6.50 a.m.	
2.50	Swindon	7.00 a.m.	
4.00	Bristol	9.35 a.m.	
4.10	Birmingham	7.00 a.m.	
4.25	Ealing Broadway	7.25 a.m.	
4.40	Paddington	8.25 a.m.	
5.25	Paddington	10.30 a.m.	*Cornish Riviera Express*
5.40	Paddington	10.35 a.m.	
6.45	Wolverhampton	8.55 a.m.	
7.00	Paddington	11.00 a.m.	
7.45	Paddington	11.05 a.m.	
8.10	Carmarthen	8.17 a.m.	
9.00	Manchester Lon. Rd.	8.00 a.m.	
9.30	Liverpool Lime	8.35 a.m.	
9.55	Paddington	1.35 p.m.	*The Royal Duchy*
10.55	Paddington	3.30 p.m.	

Summer Saturday departures from Penzance in 1959:

Depart		Arrive	
6.00	Manchester Lon. Rd.	6.15 p.m.	
7.30	Bristol	2.07 p.m.	
8.20	Paddington	5.15 p.m.	
10.00	Paddington	5.20 p.m.	*Cornish Riviera Express*
10.05	Manchester Lon. Rd.	9.55 p.m.	
10.20	Swansea	7.45 p.m.	
10.45	Sheffield	10.43 p.m.	
11.10	Wolverhampton	8.35 p.m.	
11.50	Paddington	7.50 p.m.	*The Royal Duchy*
12.00	Manchester Lon. Rd.,	2.02 a.m.	
	Glasgow Central	7.30 a.m.	
1.20	Paddington	9.05 p.m.	
4.50	Manchester Lon. Rd.	6.39 a.m.	Sleeper from Plymouth
7.05	Manchester Vic.	7.59 a.m.	
8.15	Paddington	5.00 a.m.	
8.45	Paddington via Bristol	7.25 a.m.	
9.30	Paddington	6.15 a.m.	Sleeper only

Local Services — Summer 1959

Penzance Departures — Weekdays

Depart		Arrive	
8.30	Hayle	8.47	School Train
8.55	Truro	10.00	
10.45	Plymouth	1.45	
1.55	Plymouth	5.18	
3.35	Truro	4.50	
4.20	Plymouth	7.00	
4.40	Truro	5.40	Fridays Only
5.45	Truro	6.50	
6.00	Truro	8.08	Via St. Ives
6.10	Truro	7.15	
7.18	Plymouth	10.40	

Penzance Arrivals — Weekdays

Depart		Arrive	
7.45	Truro	8.45	
6.50	Plymouth	9.50	
10.40	Truro	11.42	
9.10	Plymouth	11.50	
11.45	Truro	12.47	
11.05	Plymouth	2.25	
4.15	Truro	5.20	
5.25	Truro	6.26	
5.50	Plymouth	7.40	
6.10	Plymouth	8.55	Mons — Thurs 27 July to 27 August

The longest through journey in Britain began at Penzance on the 12.00 midday service conveying through coaches to Glasgow. It gave the unfortunate traveller a four hour journey to Plymouth alone, largely because it was a mixed passenger and parcels service, normally conveying more parcel vans than coaches. No. 6837 *Forthampton Grange* is seen here pulling away from Marazion on 23rd September 1959 on the long, slow haul northward.

P.Q. Treloar

The Mail departed Penzance at 7.00 p.m. during the last years of steam. It is seen here at St Erth reflecting the evening sun. A branch train to St Ives waits in the bay to connect with the 7.20 p.m. service from Penzance to Plymouth. *P.Q. Treloar*

Penzance shed finally closed to steam in September 1962. Two roads at the depot had long since been separated off for diesel maintenance, leaving the two remaining roads nearest the main line to house the steam power. By 1962 the latter as separate accommodation was in a marked state of deterioration falling rapidly into disuse. The last steam hauled train from Penzance was, oddly enough, 34023 *Blackmore Vale*, a Southern West Country Pacific. This headed a special working on Sunday 3rd May 1964. Chocolate and cream livery had also disappeared since 1962.

These were all visible changes as, indeed, was the closure of the Helston branch to passengers in November 1962. It underlined the sense of threat that was growing over the future of the railway in West Cornwall. The publication of the Beeching Report in 1963 served to confirm fears for the worst. In its most extreme form the long term proposals were for the closure of the entire system west of Plymouth. In the event there was a reprieve, but not without specific economies. The St. Ives branch was reduced to a spartan existence by 1964 deprived of sidings run-round loop and all freight traffic. There was also a proposal to close St. Erth station and serve the branch from Hayle, but fortunately St. Erth and the stations on the line have survived.

Actual closure did take place at Marazion. The station closed from 5th October 1964 after 112 years service. In 1945 the signal box at the station was open from 5.30 a.m. to 10.30 p.m., or, until the passing of the 2.40 p.m. goods from Tavistock Junction (Plymouth) to Ponsandane. This train was known locally as the 'Snaily' on account of its slow progress through Cornwall, and its numerous shunting operations at stations and yards en route. During the 1950s the box was worked on two shifts and one of the

signalmen was also the organist in the church at St. Michael's Mount. The other now lives at Long Rock. Marazion box was designated class 4 and was fitted with twenty-eight levers. One of these controlled the 'down' distant signal at Rospeath, (eastward beyond the marsh) which was sited well over a thousand yards from the box, at the maximum allowed distance for a manually operated lever.

There was always plenty of activity for the signalmen. Apart from heavy traffic at the yard, which had its own shunting staff, the sidings along the marsh were in constant use storing coaching stock from Penzance. Marazion sidings, including the yard space, proved invaluable for empty stock accommodation on summer Saturdays. The main line was also busy. All double-headed 'down' trains were required to stop at Marazion in order to detach the pilot locomotive, to prevent congestion at Penzance station. A long double-headed train would not necessarily clear the points at the terminus, nor could the locomotives use the crossover serving platforms 2 and 3. When the pilot was detached at Marazion, it was either sent on ahead to the depot, or was held in the 'down' refuge sidings, behind the box, and followed later. These particular sidings also received the wagons detached from 'down' freight workings through Ponsandane. This was also done to avoid the delays that would otherwise have followed from shunting across the 'up' line into the main yard.

The box was not open on Sundays other than to deal with seasonal flower traffic. On occasion this called for it to be manned for a short period at midday to enable the train to make use of the 'down' platform if loading was particularly heavy. By 1966, however, all such activity belonged to the past as in that year the box closed and operations at the yard were ended.

THE CORNISHMAN

RESTAURANT CAR SERVICE
BETWEEN
WOLVERHAMPTON, BIRMINGHAM, GLOUCESTER, BRISTOL
AND THE
WEST OF ENGLAND
Via Stratford-upon-Avon

WEEK DAYS
MONDAYS TO FRIDAYS
(For Services on Saturdays see Table 35)

		am	am			am	am
WOLVERHAMPTON (Low Level)	..dep	9 A 0	9 A 0	PENZANCE	..dep	10A30	10A30
Bilston Central	..	9 A 6	9 A 6	St. Erth	..	10A40	10A40
Wednesbury Central	..	9A12	9A12	Truro	..	11A20	11A20
West Bromwich	..	9A20	9A20	St. Austell	..	11 48	11 48
Birmingham (Snow Hill)	..	9A40	9A40	Par	..	11 57	11 57
Stratford-upon-Avon	..	10 19	10 19			pm	pm
Cheltenham Spa (Malvern Rd)	..	11 2	11 2	Plymouth	..	1 20	1 20
Gloucester Eastgate	..	11 20	11 20				
		pm	pm	Kingswear	..	12A15	
Bristol (Temple Meads)	..arr	12 15		Churston (for Brixham)	..	12A30	
Taunton	..	1 15		Goodrington Sands Halt	..	12 40	
Exeter (St. David's)	..	1 58		Paignton	..	12A55	B
Dawlish	..	2 33		Torquay	..	1 A 2	
Teignmouth	..	2 41		Torre	..	1 7	
Newton Abbot	..	2 51		Kingskerswell	..	1 15	
Torre	..	3 11		Newton Abbot	..	1 23	
Torquay	..	3 14		Teignmouth	..	1 34	B
Paignton	..	3 24		Dawlish	..	1 42	
Goodrington Sands Halt	..	3 27		Exeter (St. David's)	..	2 24	
Churston (for Brixham)	..	3 34		Taunton	..	3 5	
Kingswear	..	3 44		Bristol (Temple Meads)	..	4 8	3 52
				Gloucester Eastgate	..arr	5 3	4 40
Plymouth	..	3 20	3 10	Cheltenham Spa (Malvern Rd)	..	5 21	5 0
Liskeard	..	3 59	3 49	Stratford-upon-Avon	..	6 2	5 50
Bodmin Road	..	4 15	4 5	Birmingham (Snow Hill)	..	6 49	6 33
Par	..	4 28	4 18	West Bromwich	..	7 4	
St. Austell	..	4 39	4 29	Wednesbury Central	..	7 12	
Truro	..	5 2	4 52	Bilston Central	..	7 18	
St. Erth	..	5 38	5 28	Wolverhampton (Low Level)	..	7 25	7 a
Penzance	..	5 50	5 40				

(Column notes at right: Runs until Thursday, 23rd July inclusive and from Monday, 24th August to Friday, 21st August inclusive / Runs Friday, 24th July to Friday, 21st August inclusive)

A—Seats can be reserved in advance on payment of a fee of 2s. 0d. per seat (see page 23).

B—See Table 169 for service on these dates.

THE ROYAL DUCHY

RESTAURANT CAR SERVICE
LONDON, EXETER, PLYMOUTH, TRURO and PENZANCE

WEEK DAYS

		E	S			E	S
		pm	pm			am	am
London (Paddington)	..dep	1A30	1A35	Penzance	..dep	11A 0	11C50
Reading General	..	2 13	2 18	Marazion	..		11C54
Westbury	..arr	3 16	3 26	St. Erth	..	11A 9	12C 2
Taunton	..	4 10	4 25	Camborne	..	11A26	12C22
Exeter (St. David's)	..	4 48	5 5	Redruth	..	11A35	12C32
Dawlish	..		5 30	Chacewater	..	11A43	..
Teignmouth	..		5 39			pm	
Newton Abbot	..	5 23	5 50	Truro	..	12A 0	12 52
				St. Austell	..	12 26	1 22
Kingskerswell	..	5 37		Par	..	12 35	..
Torre	..	5 45		Lostwithiel	..	12 47	1 40
Torquay	..	5 48		Bodmin Road	..	12 56	..
Paignton	..	6 1		Liskeard	..	1 17	2 8
Goodrington Sands Halt	..	6 5		Plymouth	..	2 0	2 50
Churston (for Brixham)	..	6 12		Totnes	..	2 38	..
Kingswear	..	6 22					
				Kingswear	..		1850
Totnes	..	5 46		Churston (for Brixham)	..		2B 0
Plymouth	..	6 25	6 55	Paignton	..		2B 9
Liskeard	..	7 5	7 35	Torquay	..		2B18
Bodmin Road	..	7 21	7 50	Torre	..		2T22
Lostwithiel	..	7 28	7 57				
Par	..	7 38	8 9	Newton Abbot	..		2 58
St. Austell	..	7 49	8 20	Teignmouth	..		2T48
Truro	..	8 12	8 45	Dawlish	..		2T55
Chacewater	..	8 27	9 0	Exeter (St. David's)	..		3 31
Redruth	..	8 38	9 10	Taunton	..		4 15
Camborne	..	8 46	9 18	Westbury	..		5 15
Gwinear Road	..	8 53	9 25	Newbury	..arr	6 2	6 38
Hayle	..	9 1	9 33	Reading General	..	6 25	7 L
St. Erth	..	9 8	9 38	London (Paddington)	..	7 15	7 50
Penzance	..	9 20	9 55				

A—Seats can be reserved in advance on payment of a fee of 2s. 0d. per seat (see page 23).

B—Mondays to Thursdays only. Note A also applies.

C—Passengers travelling by this train beyond Plymouth are required to hold Regulation Tickets (see page 32). See also Note A

E—Except Saturdays

S—Saturdays only

T—Mondays to Thursdays only

Extracts from the published timetable: Summer 1959, *The Cornishman* and *The Royal Duchy*.

The Royal Duchy passing Marazion behind No. 6869 *Resolven Grange* on 6th April 1959. This was one of the new titled trains introduced in the late 1950s with chocolate and cream coaching stock. *The Cornishman* was another similar development of the time. *The Royal Duchy* left Penzance at 11 a.m. arriving Paddington at 7.15 p.m. The 'down' service departed Paddington at 1.30 p.m. arriving at Penzance at 9.20 p.m.: a poor man's *Cornish Riviera Express!*

P.Q. Treloar

Modified 'Hall' class No. 6988 *Swithland Hall* passes Marazion with the 'down' morning parcels empties including milk and gas tanks. The signalbox roof can be seen above the locomotive cab and the 'down' refuge sidings are visible on the extreme right alongside the beach. 11th May 1959.

M. Mensing

An express freight of merchandise and perishible traffic displaying the appropriate head code leaves St Erth for the east behind No. 6845 *Paviland Grange*. The well stocked sidings reflect a complete contrast with today's scene. *P.Q. Treloar*

By 1960 diesel power was common on all important services to and from West Cornwall. In this view two class '22' series locomotives wait to depart with the 6.20 p.m. milk for Kensington. It would call also at St Erth, Pengegon (Camborne) and Lostwithiel to pick up more milk tanks. An earlier service also left Penzance at 12.20 p.m. The Royal Mail stock stands behind it on Platform 4. Note the greatly increased space made available in 1937 by claiming land from the sea. *P.Q. Treloar*

It is also interesting to note that Lord St. Levan, of St. Michael's Mount enjoyed shooting rights across the line, and through the yard. Access was extended to beaters, shooters and 'any invited guns'; the signalman being informed of their presence when necessary!

Before the run-down and closure of the goods shed at Ponsandane in 1978, Penzance enjoyed a regular freight service. The working pattern in 1959 included the following: 2.50 p.m. Penzance – Paddington express goods; 5.05 p.m. Marazion – Crewe, (often referred to locally as 'the Oxley'), express service; 8.40 p.m. Paddington – Penzance; 9.40 p.m. Bristol – Penzance. Two milk trains left Penzance each day, at 12.20 p.m. and 6.20 p.m. On Sundays the trains departed at 12.35 p.m. and 5.40 p.m. The regular destination was Kensington, and loadings for the milk trains, with each full tanker of 3,000 gallons, at 28 tons were: 500 tons for a Castle locomotive, 465 tons for a Hall or Grange, and 450 tons for a Manor or 4300 Mogul. Empties were worked down with the morning parcels, which included the gas tanks from Truro to replenish the dining and sleeping cars. For reasons of safety, gas vehicles were always located at the rear of the train in the event of damage or leakage. Perishable and parcels traffic was conveyed on both the 12.00 Penzance –Glasgow, largely a mixed working of passenger coaches and vans, and the 2.00 p.m. 'Perishable' to Crewe. The Glasgow service at midday was virtually a stopping train to Plymouth giving the unfortunate passenger a 3½ hour journey overall from Penzance. Another typical service of the time was the 4.10 p.m. meat train from Penzance. The actual meat vans, 'Insul-meat' were scrubbed and cleaned in the most scrupulous manner by staff at Penzance before loading took place, ensuring a spotless interior. Cylindrical ice bags were also used in these vans to chill the meat and were fitted by means of a special access in the roof.

By contrast, today, freight traffic is almost non-existent. The ex-GWR goods shed is derelict and the only traffic to use Ponsandane yard consists of oil fuel tanks for the depot and permanent way trains when required. Cement wagons from the plant at Chacewater travel down to Penzance in order to remove empty tankers and to reverse, there being no crossover between the cement depot at Chacewater and Long Rock. This train runs as required, invariably arriving at Long Rock during the mid morning and returning eastward soon after. Until 1983 a freight service worked between Ponsandane yard and Hayle wharves conveying fuel and chemical traffic. This worked in connection with an I.C.I. plant, and providing useful revenue. It has since ceased, and the track on its 1 in 30 gradient down to the wharf has been lifted. The signal box at Hayle station, controlling the line, has also been demolished.

Over the last decade there have also been many changes to the railway facilities along the shoreline at Penzance. Marazion was by no means the only closure. In 1974 the line was singled from a point immediately east of Long Rock occupation crossing at milepost 325 to Penzance station in connection with new developments. These included an H.S.T. and coach servicing depot at Long Rock, new signalling arrangements, and detailed alterations to the track.

Both Long Rock and Ponsandane signal boxes were demolished in the latter part of 1974, and all signalling was then controlled from Penzance box. Long Rock box controlled movements to and from the locomotive depot and the eastern end of the yard from Ponsandane. Following the Second World War, it was operated from 5.30 a.m. to Midnight, or the passage of the last locomotive to the shed, whilst on Sundays it was worked from 6.05 a.m. to 10.05 p.m. This box also controlled a short siding, immediately opposite, which was rented by the Shell Oil

The Western Region's early main line diesel locomotives, the Type 4 'Warship' Class North British D600s entered service in May 1958. These five locomotives were not a great success and were soon superceded by another much lighter Swindon and North British product, the D800 series. D604 *Cossack* is seen here entering Penzance with the 'down' *Cornish Riviera Express* in April 1960. The locomotive from this train returned eastward with the *Royal Mail* during the evening, leaving at 7 p.m. *P.Q. Treloar*

D800 *Sir Brian Robertson*, first of the Swindon-built diesel hydraulics, leaves Penzance on the 10.00 a.m. *Cornish Riviera Express* on 23rd September 1959. The train is passing the site of the former timber viaduct replaced in 1921 by the embankment shown here. Note the Royal Mail set in the 'slopers sidings' alongside the train. *P.Q. Treloar*

Company who had a small oil terminus there. Long Rock box also controlled the crossing to the beach, the gates being operated manually by a large wheel.

Ponsandane box with its flat roof (a legacy from legislation of the 1870s) controlled the west side of Ponsandane yard including the four platform faces for goods traffic and the eastern entrance/exit to the sloper's siding on the 'up' side of the main line, reaching towards the terminus. The box was fitted with thirty levers and also gave gated access for vehicles to the beach. When these boxes closed both the crossings were protected by automatic barriers operated from Penzance, until the winter of 1984, when Ponsandane crossing was closed to traffic and replaced by a wooden footbridge.

Penzance locomotive depot closed during the latter part of 1976 and demolition was in progress by January 1977. This continued throughout the winter months until the site was eventually levelled and it is now no more than wasteland awaiting possible redevelopment. The HST depot has been built alongside this site next to the main line. Construction began here in 1976 on the single road accommodation, immediately east of the former good shed. New carriage sidings were also provided in conjunction with the depot, on land between the latter and Long Rock crossing to the east. Five lines of siding were eventually installed to store HST sets overnight along with coaching stock, the Royal Mail and the 'Sleeper'. General cleaning and servicing is also carried out here. To the west of the new depot an automatic washing plant has also been built. Access to this and the new depot is gained over the old 'up' line which now runs into Ponsandane yard.

A resignalling programme formed part of the new arrangements between Penzance and Marazion, with coloured lights, operated from Penzance box, replacing all semaphore signals as far as St. Erth where, outwardly, little other than motive power

and the removal of the yard has changed since the pre-Beeching era.

Reference to St. Erth gives the opportunity to record the demise of milk traffic from the yard in 1980. All movement was from that time transferred to road transport and the yard was lifted.

Train services in 1959, as outlined earlier, represented the pre-Beeching era. Consideration of the timetable for 1969 gives the opportunity for comparisons and contrast.

One of the major developments of May 1969 was the abandonment of the practice, introduced in 1962, of including both Torbay and Plymouth/Penzance portions in all services to the west. *The Cornish Riviera* achieved its first ever 3½ hour schedule from Paddington to Plymouth, stopping only at Exeter. Journey time to Penzance was cut back to 5 hours 35 minutes. Departure time from Paddington was 10.30 a.m. and from Penzance at 11.25 a.m. (limited accommodation only on seat reservation).

The Cornishman, now the only other named train linked with Penzance, was retimed and accelerated over the route to and from Bradford. On the 'up' service, departure from Penzance was at 9.50 a.m. arriving at Bradford at 20.06. The corresponding service departed Bradford at 7.06 a.m. and arrived at Penzance at 17.17. (these were the weekday timings).

On the West of England main line, there were five daytime services from Penzance to Paddington other than the Sleeper services on weekdays. These were timed to depart at 7.25 a.m., 9.15 a.m., 11.25 a.m., 13.15 and 15.20. From Paddington departures were: 8.30 a.m., 10.30 a.m., 12.30, 14.30 and 16.30. The 7.25 a.m. from Penzance and the 12.30 from Paddington covered the 305¼ miles in 6 hours dead; the best performances, other than the Cornish Riviera itself.

Summer Saturday arrivals at Penzance in 1969:

Arrive		Depart	
05.10	Sheffield	19.20	FRI. (14 June — 29 Aug). Newcastle dep. 16.15 FRI. (4 July — 22 Aug).
05.40	Paddington	22.55	Sleeping accommodation for Isles of Scilly passengers only. First and second class coaches also.
07.52	Paddington	00.55	Sleeping Car accommodation only.
08.35	Paddington	23.30	via Bristol and Weston-Super-Mare
09.25	Paddington	23.45	Sleeper service via Bristol
10.05	Liverpool Lime St	23.50	
11.40	Exeter	07.15	
12.30	Manchester Picc	00.50	
13.45	St. Ives	13.15	
14.25	Oxford	07.08	
14.50	Ealing Broadway	07.37	
15.15	Paddington	08.30	
16.10	Wolverhampton H.L.	08.08	
16.50	Paddington	10.30	*Cornish Riviera Express*
17.30	Cardiff	10.35	
17.50	Bradford	07.06	*The Cornishman*
18.25	Paddington	11.30	
19.05	Manchester Picc.	09.05	via Severn Tunnel
19.25	Paddington	12.30	
21.15	Paddington	14.30	
23.10	Paddington	16.30	

Summer Saturday Departures from Penzance in 1969 included the following:

Depart		Arrive	
6.10	Paddington	13.15	
7.45	Liverpool Lime St	17.35	
8.15	Paddington	15.20	
8.45	Wolverhampton H.L.	17.20	
9.30	Bradford	20.06	*The Cornishman*
9.50	Manchester Picc.	19.44	
10.15	Paddington	16.30	*Cornish Riviera Express*
10.45	Paddington	18.00	
11.20	Leeds City	22.06	
12.35	Paddington	19.35	
13.30	Liverpool Lime St	01.14	
14.30	St. Ives	14.52	
15.20	Paddington	21.30	
16.20	Newton Abbot	19.56	
17.55	Manchester Picc.	05.27	
19.00	Plymouth	21.25	
21.00	Paddington	07.00	Sleeper via Bristol
21.30	Paddington	05.30	via Westbury route
22.00	Paddington	05.50	Sleeper only.

Conclusion

The railway plays an important part in the social and economic life of West Cornwall and therefore must be subject to the inevitable process of adaption and change. Having left the story of the terminus as it stood in 1985 it is now necessary to update events.

Early in 1987 the station lost its loading bays and general accommodation for perishable traffic that had long been a feature of the terminus. Much of this area immediately south of platform four is now under redevelopment, a new tourist information centre appearing in the station yard. All of this serves to underline the emphasis put upon tourism and passenger travel generally.

One of the high points of the new timetable is the much publicised 'Cornishman' service now running to and from Newcastle. Under IC 125 working, the train departs Penzance at 7.30 am with a journey time to Newcastle of 8 hours 54 minutes. Southbound, the service leaves Newcastle at 11.25 am with arrival at Penzance at 20.02. A good deal of local and national publicity was given to this train on its first day. In particular, the BBC's 'Blue Peter' programme covered the event, naming the leading Inter City power car 'Blue Peter II' on the southward run. Another interesting service, 'The Cornish Scot', provides a fast through working to and from Glasgow and Edinburgh,

giving further indication of a positive commitment to the future of the railway locally. The southbound working leaves Glasgow at 7.20 am and Edinburgh at 7.14; arrival time at Penzance being 18.40.

Freight traffic plays little part in the local railway scene today but the tradition of the 'Holiday Line' is still very much apparent. Cornwall's varied and magnificent landscape is well able to attract tourists in numbers, despite the tremendous increase in foreign competition. St Michael's Mount, the show-piece of Great Western publicity over the years, continues to excite rail travellers as today's trains glide across the marshlands to the shoreline and journey's end; likewise, the branch line to St Ives, terminating above the sands of Porthminster Beach, treats passengers en route to one of the most spectacular railway journeys in Britain. The mythology of the 'Cornish Riviera' or 'Ocean Coast' has substance in West Cornwall and the reality of holiday trains running along the seashore will, hopefully, remain with us for many years to come. Indeed, with well over a century of service, locally, the railway has itself become an intrinsic part of the community it serves. It has a distinguished history, and effective contemporary presence and, we can only assume, therefore, a positive future.

I would like the book to carry a dedication:
'To my father (D.W.B.), who liked trains.'

Acknowledgements

I would like to thank the following for all their help and interest in the preparation of this book. Firstly, Roger Hardingham for allowing me the opportunity to develop the work and for his concern and advice throughout. Terry Knight and the Staff of the Local Studies Library, have, as always, been exceptionally helpful, as indeed have Mr H.L. Douch and the Staff of the Royal Institution of Cornwall; the Staff of the Reference room – Penzance Public Library; The Penzance Library, Morrab Park; Penlee House Museum, Penzance, and the Cornwall County Record Office at Truro.

Individually, I must thank Mr Ron Edhouse of Long Rock, ex-signalman at Marazion Station, for his invaluable information relating to train workings there; Mr J. Harris, for extensive information on freight services at Penzance under GWR and BR ownership; the late Mr Bill Saunders of Long Rock for his recollections as a railway guard in the area; Mr R. Winnen and Mr G. Corin for timetables both ancient and modern, and Mr A. Leeds for details on current matters concerning the permanent way.

With regard to the illustrations I must thank Mr P. Treloar, Mr P. Gray and Mr M. Mensing for their excellent photographs covering the period since the World War Two; also the good services of the Local Studies Library at Redruth, the Royal Institution at Truro and Penlee House Museum at Penzance.

Many thanks also to Margaret Barron for typing the manuscript and dealing cheerfully with numerous alterations and additions. Finally thanks to my wife, Jo, for interest above and beyond the call of duty in terms of railways past and present.